COMMUNION
THROUGH
PREACHING

OMMUNION
THROUGH
PREACHING

THE MONSTRANCE OF THE GOSPEL

The George Craig Stewart Lectures on Preaching at
Seabury-Western Theological Seminary, Evanston, Illinois

by

HENRY SLOANE COFFIN

President-Emeritus
of Union Theological Seminary,
New York City

1952

CHARLES SCRIBNER'S SONS, NEW YORK
CHARLES SCRIBNER'S SONS, LTD., LONDON

Dedicated

with Admiration and Affection

to

Frederick Clifton Grant

Ecumenical Churchman
President of Seabury-Western Theological
Seminary, 1927–38
Edward Robinson Professor of Biblical Theology
at
Union Theological Seminary, New York City,
since 1938

PREFACE

In the autumn of 1951 the Faculty of Seabury-Western Theological Seminary did me the honor to ask me to deliver four lectures on Preaching upon the George Craig Stewart Foundation. The substance of those lectures is in the chapters of this brief volume.

Several of my friends in the Protestant Episcopal Church had lamented to me of a waning interest in preaching among the younger ministers. This has apparently accompanied the increased emphasis upon the Holy Communion and the frequency of its celebration. In several cities where formerly during Lent weeks of daily preaching had been customary, this practice had been abandoned and instead several celebrations of the Communion had been substituted. However, in all instances of which I had figures the attendance was much less. Hence I decided to approach the theme of preaching by showing that both sermons and the Supper of the Lord are means of grace and media through which God in Christ offers Himself in personal fellowship.

Bishop Stewart, in whose honor the lectureship had been founded, was a very eloquent and moving preacher. He had been born and reared in the Methodist Church, and carried over with him into the Episcopal Communion the tradition of fervid evangelistic preaching of his earlier training. This was a large factor in his potent influence as bishop. It is not likely that he, Anglo-Catholic as were his later sympathies, would have disparaged preaching. In any case, without belittling either sermon or sacrament, it is plain that historically in the tradition of all Churches which are heirs of the Sixteenth-Century Reformation both belong together. It is the main point of these chapters to encourage sacramental sermons—sermons which enable God to have face to face Communion with His people. I am indebted to Dean Kelley, his associates on the faculty, and to the students for their kindly reception of one who came to them from the Presbyterian Church where our Reformed worship exalts the sermon as the chief factor in the public worship of Almighty God.

H. S. C.

TABLE OF CONTENTS

COMMUNION
THROUGH
PREACHING

THE WORD AND THE
SACRAMENTS

*"*B<small>E</small> <small>THOU</small> a faithful Dispenser of the Word of God and of his holy Sacraments" runs the charge in the Ordination Service in the *Book of Common Prayer*. This coupling of the Word and Sacraments prevails in all Churches of the Reformation. Both belong in the definition of the Church, and in the description of her ministry.

Both Word and Sacraments mediate God's communion with His responsive people. In both, therefore, He is contemporaneously present with them. In both He encounters us face to face. In the Lord's Supper we believe Him to be both Host and Food—*Hospes atque Epulum*. In His preached Word, He is both Speaker and Message. We preach Christ the power of God and the wisdom of God. And in the act of preaching it is not alone we, poor stammering ambassadors and faulty interpreters, who speak—"as though God did beseech you by us, we pray you in Christ's stead, Be ye reconciled to God."

There is much current disparagement of preaching, and that among some of the more thoughtful in our churches. A noted preacher and colleague of mine, the late Dr. Johnston Ross, spoke some years ago of "the uninterrupted garrulity of Protestant worship." There is hardly an occasion when God's people assemble at which a minister does not feel called upon to make some "remarks"—a shallow noun which the dictionary interprets by equally superficial words, "a notice, note, or comment; an observation." It is a wholesome reassertion of the priesthood of all believers when Christians protest against this widespread loquacious clericalism. A pamphleteer in the Restoration Period in England attributed the prevalent low opinion of the Church and her ministry in large part to the "knack in preaching." The mid-seventeenth century had acquired a glibness in talk upon religious themes. The pamphleteer went on to say:

"Unless a man be excessively dull, he can, without warning, lay hold of any text in Scripture, and tear and tumble it until the hour-glass run out."

Today, notices, prayers, the announcement of a hymn or of the offering open an occasion for ministerial chat. Even the benediction may be deferred for a minute to remind the impatient congregation of some forthcoming event which has escaped their pastor's attention. Is it any wonder that amid this spate of clerical verbosity there should be pleas for services without sermons? Or that the administration of a sacrament, with its own inherent divinely fixed message, should be preferred as a medium for God's fellowship? This is a natural revolt from the voluble occupants of American pulpits.

Note, however, that this is a twentieth-century revolt. In the sixteenth century, after public worship had long been generally destitute of preaching, a sermon was insisted upon as its safeguard from meaningless magic. The English *Book of Common Prayer* of 1549 in its office of Holy Communion has a rubric which reads peremptorily, "after the Creed ended shall follow the sermon." By and large, the reformers, embattled against a degradation of worship, insisted that the Word must be linked with the Sacraments so that fellowship with God might become reasonable, the meeting of Person with persons, minds, hearts, consciences awake and in accord. This was a return to New Testament Christianity. In the sixth chapter of St. John's gospel, Christ's "flesh and blood"—by that date surely taken as an allusion to the Holy Supper—seem synonymous with His words: "the words that I speak unto you, they are spirit and they are life," and parallels "whoso eateth my flesh and drinketh my blood hath eternal life."

One still sees services announced in the press, "Public Worship and Sermon," as though the sermon were not an integral element of public worship. To be sure, the notice in the Saturday paper may be a not inaccurate description of what is to be presented the following morning. A talk on current events, or on some social evil, or on managing one's feelings, escaping one's worries, or overcoming fears, on "integrating one's personality"—the whole range of social and psychological disquisition—is hardly the vehicle for the personal approach of Almighty God eliciting adoration, trust and love. It is told of the unfortunate Louis XVI that one day on leaving church he remarked to an attendant: "If the good abbé had talked a little about religion, I think he would have mentioned everything." God has a correspondingly inconspicuous role in many sermons of our time. He rates a single rather perfunctory reference in the final paragraph, as in the public utterances of our statesmen. The leaders of the sixteenth-century Reformation, let alone the prophets and apostles, would consider many modern preachers degenerate successors. For them God met His people in His Word, and met them redeemingly. The chief point in preaching was to supply this encounter of God with the souls of men. He must Himself be the object of their concentrated attention, of their outgoing affection, of their surrendered wills. The coupling of Word and Sacrament makes this plain. What must be restored in the Church is such "sacramental" preaching. To employ Dr. Carnegie Simpson's metaphor we must set forth Christ in "the monstrance of the Gospel."

We may well dwell further on this comparison of preached Word and Sacrament. If it be not irreverent to pry into holy things, where is God present and at work in the Sacraments? Is He to be thought of as becoming resident in the physical symbols—in the water of Baptism, in the consecrated Bread and Cup on the Table? Large sections of Christendom believe that. But does it comport with Him who is Spirit, and therefore personal in all His dealings with His children, our Father, Redeemer, Friend, to manifest Himself in sub-personal symbols? No one would disparage symbols made such by Christ Himself, and which convey to us the thought of His own mind, the affection of His heart, the very touch of His unseen hand. But is it not more correct, more congruous with God's Self-revelation in the Scriptures, to speak of Him as present in the entire action of the Sacraments? Sacraments are corporate acts of the Church, Christ's Body. The physical symbols derive their contemporary power from the Church which celebrates them in Christ's name, and through which

He Himself, alive and active, participates in their celebration. The action of the Church in Baptism is inseparably linked with Christ's presence and becomes a means of His grace, a medium through which He Himself, and none other, graciously admits us to the fellowship of His believing people, dowers us with His Holy Spirit, and assures the newcomer of his inheritance of the treasures in the Church of all the ages. In the corporate action of Baptism with all its elements—the physical symbol of water, the fellowship of believers present, the saints of many centuries whom they represent on the current scene, the hallowed words, conferring the name of God in Christ—the living, invisible Lord of the Church acts. Similarly in the Supper He is personally with His followers and reveals Himself (to employ a New Testament expression) in "the breaking of the bread." Note the verb of action—"in the breaking."

Throughout the Scriptures, God discloses Himself in events, in mighty and compassionate acts in human affairs. In the call of a solitary patriarch to take his family and possessions upon a long and venturesome journey; in the mysterious moving of the conscience of a lawgiver to enact a loftier righteousness for his people; in the advance of clans of tribesmen to take possession of a land and set up a more just and fraternal society; in the defeats of apostate monarchs, and in the summons by prophets to repentance and godlier life, above all, in the birth, life, teaching, cross, and resurrection of Jesus of Nazareth, God acts. Responsive spirits recognize His presence, interpret His activity, communicate their interpretation to a community, the Church, which conserves and abundantly utters the memory of God's goodness. That Church transmits her evangel in symbolic rites, like the Passover and the Supper of the Lord, and proclaims it in her prophetic message. She becomes a messenger to the nations, a light to lighten the Gentiles.

In Christian corporate worship there is an element of memory—the recollection of God's mighty deeds on His people's behalf—but memory is merely a prelude to His present fellowship with them. In the Supper of the Lord this factor of memory is basic: "This do in remembrance of Me." The broken loaf, the out-poured wine, derive their meaning from a momentous event in ancient Jerusalem. It is an occurrence in the stream of human history: He "suffered under Pontius Pilate, was crucified, dead, and buried. The third day He rose again." And in the community of believers brought into being by that occurrence of a distant past, the memory of these happenings in history becomes the vehicle in the present for God's manifestation of Himself to His believing people. He continues to be known of them in "the breaking of the bread." So is it also with the preaching of His Word. That

Word was given in historic happenings and in their spiritual consequences for individuals and for the people of God. His Church has sifted and conserved her recollections of these events in the Holy Scriptures. All her preachers must start from her historic memories. If they do not, there is danger that they proclaim "another gospel," not the authentic tidings of God's Self-revelation in that particular spiritual history which reached its climax in the Word made flesh in Jesus and in the Church which His redemptive mission brought into life. But in preaching, as in the Holy Supper, memory is the prelude to a contemporary Self-manifestation of the living God to His people. It is this immediate fellowship of God in Christ with man for which every sermon must furnish the occasion.

Where is God present in the preaching of the Word? Is He in the moving content of the message? Assuredly, provided that message embodies the Gospel. Is He present in the life and character of the preacher? We recall Phillips Brooks' familiar definition of preaching as "truth through personality." Is He in the company of worshipping people, the Church, the Body of the Spirit? Those of us who have tried to preach to a crowd of casual passers-by on a street corner or to a group in a non-Christian land, know the vast difference between the faces of these apathetically curious folk and those of sympathetic worshipping believers. As in

the Sacrament, is not God present in the whole
action of the Church? In the hallowed message
which has been transmitted by Him in the past?
In the dedicated life of His minister? In the company looking towards the pulpit, and seeming to
say, as did Cornelius to Simon Peter at Caesarea:
"Now therefore are we all here present before God
to hear all things that are commanded thee of God"?
The preaching of the Word is a corporate action in
which preacher, congregation, a long line of their
predecessors reaching back through the centuries
to the original event and corroborating the interpretation given that event in the Scripture, co-operate.
And God is present and active in them all to speak
to the man or woman for whom His spirit is seeking.

True preaching, like the Sacrament of the Holy
Supper, has both a Godward and a manward aspect. In the Prayer of Consecration in the *Book of
Common Prayer*, you begin with the Oblation—the
offering to God of this memorial prescribed by
Jesus Himself, and so in accordance with God's
mind. Similarly, the preacher prepares and presents
to God a sermon containing His word authenticated
time and again as His redeeming power—a sermon
through which God may address directly the hearts
and consciences of a congregation. In the preparation of the sermon, the minister must think pri-
marily of the suitableness to God of his offering.

Let him begin with an oblation. This is lost sight of in much discussion of homiletics. The emphasis is upon the "life situations" of the congregation, the capture of their attention, the stirring of their emotions, the kindling of their imaginations, the grip upon their consciences. All of this is important and dare not be neglected. But it remains secondary to the oblation to God of a sermon through which He, the Father of our Lord Jesus Christ, can congenially speak and reveal Himself movingly to His sons and daughters. Let the preacher ask himself—Is this message appropriate for God in Christ? Is it after His heart, in conformity with His mind, an utterance of His conscience who is the wellspring of eternal righteousness? To be sure, it starts from God's Self-disclosure in some past event—in a revealing incident, in a transforming word, in the struggle of a soul generations ago, in the doubts, frustrations, obstinate questionings which beset a nation in tragedy, in the trust, resolves, sacrifices of those who with God overcame their hindrances and were matured by His painful discipline. If a minister confidently believes that God has spoken, that He may speak again and through him, he will determine to align himself with the historically given Word of God, and preach naught incongruous with it. Hence, his every sermon will be grounded in Scripture and bring the message of an ancient day to bear on current needs. That anchors

it securely in the revelation of God in His dealings
with Israel and in His full disclosure of Himself
in Jesus.

As one glances over the topics which ministers
advertise as themes of their messages, how often one
questions whether through this form of thought
and speech the God of patriarchs and prophets, the
Father of our Lord Jesus Christ, can make His
judgments and His redeeming love felt and known.
Has the would-be preacher kept his eyes on God in
the preparation of the sermon, to render it a fitting
means of His Self-communication to His children?

This stress on the Godward aspect of a sermon
is not to overlook its manward side. It is a message
from and about God to a particular company of
men, women and children, who are committed to
this pastor's care with their distinctive sins, weak-
nesses and aspirations. It would be inappropriate
for their discerning Father were it not strikingly
relevant to their spiritual necessities. The preacher
must hold God and this congregation of His people
together in one thought if in Christ's stead God
through his sermon is to pray them "Be ye reconciled to Me." One may expatiate on an accurate
diagnosis of their cases and on the skilful phrasing
of the message to catch their minds so that the sermon speaks directly to their condition. But their
condition cannot be made primary. The minister is
not a physician equipped with an ample pharma-

copoeia, from which he takes remedies for their varied ills. He is the personal envoy of the all-sufficient God; and his sole aim is to let God draw near in His Word and minister out of His unsearchable riches to needs which He, and He alone, fully understands. His sermon must be an expression of the good news of God, and good news which God Himself speaks in the conscience of each listener.

In the process of sermon writing, the condition of the congregation may well come first. It must, if the sermon is to be relevant. There is much to be said for letting the first few sentences be a description of the contemporary social situation or the present mood of some hearer and then introducing a Scripture passage which met a similar situation or mood. That assures the Word of God in the Bible becoming alive today, and not seeming a matter of far-off times. Gripping sermons always convey this feeling of the immediacy of the need to which they are addressed and of the present God eager to find His children, where they are at the moment. But the order of the process of sermon composition does not alter the primary purpose to furnish God with a means of meeting His people.

To have at hand the passage of Scripture which fits the situation to which the sermon is directed, a minister must become an assiduous collector of texts. Somewhere within the ample frontiers of the Canon there is a passage for every purpose which a Christian sermon may be framed to meet. Unhappily, even among theological students and ministers there is widespread ignorance of the content of the Bible. This is crippling to the would-be preacher. Many ministers confine themselves to a small range of the Bible. Their texts are familiar. But it is often from the less pulpit-worn parts of Scripture that the most arresting starts of sermons can be made. The element of novelty grips attention.

Let me illustrate from a very common state of mind. The cult of naturalism is widespread among us. Since the majority of our people became urban, it is customary to look on nature romantically. This was not the case when farmers viewed it practically as the source of their livelihood, nor would it be so thought of did we live in the tropics or near the poles where man is obliged to battle with nature for survival. No such poetry as Wordsworth's would have been produced in the Arctic or at the equator. But for city dwellers in the temperate zones in a machine civilization, growing things possess an aesthetic fascination and this leads easily to a semireligious nature worship, further encouraged by the current passion for psychiatry as the healer of man's ills—a cult which abhors moral condemnation and stresses adjustment to things as they are. This cult of naturalism is no new thing. The prophets of Israel battled with it. Ezekiel writes:

"And he brought me into the inner court of the Lord's house, and, behold, at the door of the temple of the Lord, between the porch and the altar, were about five and twenty men, with their backs toward the temple of the Lord, and their faces toward the east; and they worshipped the sun toward the east." (8:16.)

How vivid this description of the apostasy of representative Israelites, "elders" they are called in a subsequent passage; they may even have been members of the priesthood from their location in the temple. We see in our time similar apostasies from ancestral church religion. A modern poet has written:

> "Forget, men, everything
> Upon this earth newborn,
> Except that it is lovelier
> Than any mysteries.
> Open your eyes to the air
> That has washed the eyes of the stars
> Through all the dewy night;
> Up with the light,
> To the old wars:
> Arise, arise!"

Nature, however lovely, can offer us only "the old wars." There is no progress in her cult. That comes from something which is brought to nature, and brought from on high.

Another text to approach this same current malady is from a writer who faced circumstances akin to those of Ezekiel. The writer of Job confesses:

"If I beheld the sun when it shined,
  Or the moon walking in brightness;
  And my heart hath been secretly enticed,
  Or my mouth hath kissed my hand:
  This also were an iniquity to be punished
    by the judges:
  For I should have denied the God that is
    above."   (31:26–28.)

"The God that is above"—this is the Gospel. He who is over all, loftier than man's loftiest, wiser than our wisest, better than our best, He alone can raise us out of nature into heavenly places wholly different from those in which we naturally think and feel and live.

Looking back over the half century in which the writer has tried to minister the Gospel, here is an outstanding difference between the beginning and the middle of this twentieth century. Then every effort seemed to be to insist on the likeness of God to man. Preachers even spoke of His "humanness," as though His similarity to ourselves were something to cheer over. This was supposed to be a main element in the religion of Jesus Himself. But how carefully, when our Lord used man as a metaphor for the Most High, He stressed His unlikeness as well as His identity. Using the illustration of a father's affection for a child as an encouragement to prayer, He concludes not "How similarly shall your heavenly Father," but "How much more shall your heavenly Father give His Holy Spirit to them that ask Him." It is that limitless *more* which characterizes everything in "the God that is above." And it is to that transcendent superiority to the highest in man that we with Christ must climb in our thinking to reach conceptions not too utterly inadequate for our Father who is in heaven. God is in history, in life as it is, for He is its faithful Creator; but He is above it, an invader from on high, as He came in His incarnate Son, and lifts it and us, His children, releasingly unto Himself. Starting from these somewhat unfamiliar texts which of themselves make plain the danger of the current involvement in nature with its old wars, we preach the God that is above, and let Him upraise His sin-bound children into adoring fellowship with Himself.

Much may be said for a return to the use of nature in its vastness as a suggestion of the mightiness of its Creator. The prophet's message to the exiles in Babylon: "Lift up your eyes on high" is needed for our disheartened generation. William Beebe, the naturalist, tells us of a ritual through which he and the late Theodore Roosevelt used to go at Sagamore Hill.

"After an evening talk, perhaps about the fringes of knowledge, or some new possibility of climbing into the minds or senses of animals, we would go out on the lawn, where we took turns in an amusing little astronomical rite. We searched until we found, with or without glasses, the faint heavenly spot of light-mist beyond the lower left-hand corner of the great square of Pegasus, when one or the other of us would recite:

'That is the Spiral Galaxy of Andromeda.
It is as large as our Milky Way.
It is one of a hundred million galaxies.
It is seven hundred and fifty thousand
    light-years away.
It consists of one hundred billion suns,
    each larger than our sun.'

After an interval, Colonel Roosevelt would grin at me and say: 'Now I think we are small enough! Let's go to bed.'"

(*The Book of Naturalists*, ed., William Beebe, p. 234.)

Or take another common mood—the feeling, prevalent in our world, of impotence. What progress can we make socially in a day when resources are being consumed for defence and young men must give their best years to military training? How many congregations, both urban and rural, find themselves in situations where growth in numbers seems impossible. The Bible shows such frustrating situations and what is to be done in them by Christian leaders. Here, for example, is the aggressive and tireless apostle to the Gentiles on a vessel which has been overwhelmed by a storm and is being beached.

"Then fearing lest we should have fallen upon rocks, they cast four anchors out of the stern, and wished for the day."

Does not that scene fit our apprehensive time? Progress may be out of the question; but it is something to anchor and hold on. Nor is nothing to be done in such circumstances. The apostle kept everyone on board: there were no crippling desertions. That is much when a vessel is about to break in pieces. And he kept up their normal life: "I pray you to take some food, for this is for your health." Maintaining those aboard in robust vigor is no small achievement. And standing before them amid threatening seas, the apostle "gave thanks to God." This is contagious faith which infected his fellow-voyagers: "Then were they all of good cheer." That scene on a stormy sea with a ship in imminent peril fits our world. The poise and courage of St. Paul, and the practical steps which he took, guide Christians today. Above all, through this scene, the living God, whose he was and whom he served, comes to us and speaks His Word to us.

This feeling of impotence is keen in the Church. We know assuredly that believers ought and can do and bear what unbelievers cannot: "By faith they went through the Red Sea as by dry land, which the Egyptians assaying to do were drowned." But the frustrations of our bewildering time, the experiences through which men and women pass, the ordeals which must be undergone seem to be met with no more conspicuous triumph by those within than by many without the Christian Church. Take as a starting-point for a relevant sermon—*Believers and Egyptians in the Same Overwhelming Circumstances.*

Our weakness and incompetence in the Church is often due to the secondhand character of our religious faith. Pastor and people live on a traditional or a hearsay religion. Like the Jewish exorcists in Ephesus, too many of us are saying: "We adjure you by Jesus whom Paul preacheth." There is an absence of firsthand knowledge, of personal fellowship, in our witness. The source of our hearsay faith may be excellent; our tradition, our heritage, our education and teachers may be of the best. One could scarcely improve upon St. Paul; but Christ's power is not transmissible to any unpossessed of direct union with Him in whom we can do all things. Isaiah complained of his contemporaries: "Their fear of me has become mere precept of men learned by rote." Jeremiah denounced prophets who have not "stood in the Council of the Lord," who gabbled the religious patter of the day, and he says grimly: "They steal everyone my words from his neighbor." His was a generation of impotent ministerial plagiarists.

With so many seated before us in defeatist mood, we may use a text which states the basic commonplace of all religion: "God is able." Has any believer ever worshipped one whom he deemed an incompetent god? The New Testament uses the phrase as a title of Deity in doxologies: "Unto Him who is able." Jude writes "Unto Him who is able to keep you from slipping"—a telling expression to describe the plight of many to whom we speak. Paul has a somewhat kindred thought when he writes to the Romans: "The Lord is able to make him stand." The apostle is discussing religious liberty and is aware of the peril that freedom will be abused. But he is confident that the grace and power of Christ enable such liberty to prove a triumphant moral success. Again he dwells in the letter to Philippi upon the adequacy of Christ "to subdue all things unto Himself." There is a tonic for hesitant Christians: "able to subdue all things unto Himself," and the preacher can specify some of the recalcitrant things in ourselves, in the thought and mood of our time, in nations and individuals on the present scene, which give us foreboding— "able to subdue all things unto Himself." Take another doxology in the Letter to the Ephesians: "Now unto Him that is able to do exceeding abundantly above all that we ask or think." How frequently we circumscribe God by our presuppositions of what He is likely to do or capable of doing! We confine Him within the boundaries of our calculations, and this limited Deity operates within our cramping expectations. No expression in Scripture emancipates faith more completely than this: "Able to do exceeding abundantly above all that we ask or think." Once again, in a letter to the Corinthians, the apostle piles up his universals, his "alls and his always": "God is able to make all grace abound toward you, that ye always having all sufficiency in all things, may abound to every good work." That, in the simplest Bible outline, is a sermon from the three words elementary in the description of God in any faith: "God is able."

Again the ministry and membership of the Church is full of earnest folk devoid of the divine energy with which the Christian Church has been athrob in all her great ages. To how many of us, both in pulpit and pew, might the question be put: "Received ye the Holy Spirit when ye believed?" Our generation has had the baptism of John. We have been out for righteousness in politics, in international relations, in industry; but despite resolute endeavors we seem to be making scant headway. Ours is largely a religion of effort, and the effort appears futile. That which has characterized the Church in her periods of power—the indwelling and outworking of the Spirit, is painfully absent from many congregations. Pastor and people may be conscientious, hard-working, ingenious in devising methods. Their church may give the impression of bustling activity; their weekly calendar lists a bewildering number of meetings, and their pastor may hang on his study wall a graph of interrelations of all these groups and win the reputation of a skilful administrator; but fruits in altered lives and homes and in spiritual influence on the community are dismally lacking. "Received ye the Holy Spirit when ye believed?" Our congregation might reply: "The Holy Spirit—why that is what they talk about in the 'fringe sects,' not in proper congregations affiliated with the National Council of the Churches of Christ in the U.S.A." Yes, and that is perhaps one reason why these fringe sects keep springing up in place after place. They have something which the more conventional churches lack. And notice in that passage in the nineteenth chapter of Acts how expectation limits experience. Pius the Ninth is said to have remarked in 1870: "Before I was pope, I *believed* in papal infallibility, now (after the Vatican Council) I *feel* it." The John-the-Baptistites at Ephesus had not heard that the Spirit was given and was the empowering possession of every Christian. They were totally unaware of Him. The apostle preached to them Jesus and all that ensues in the new life in the Church in Him, with the result that "the Holy Ghost came upon them; and they spake with tongues and prophesied." That was a first-century manifestation of the Spirit, and the twentieth is not confined to that pattern. The point is that expectation enabled the already given Spirit to work and the signs of His presence became patent.

There are two kinds of spiritual energy, corresponding to dynamic and static forms of physical energy—the force to do and the force to endure. For years from my study window on Morningside Heights, I looked up the Hudson River to the George Washington Bridge. It offered me a constant view of these two varieties of energy. There was the steady stream of motor vehicles—trucks, busses, cars of all sorts—crossing back and forth from Manhattan Island to New Jersey. They disclosed power in action for the business of mankind. And there was that vast structure of steel upheld by miles and miles of wire no bigger than one's little finger—enough of it to girdle our globe four times and more—on which the roadway with its tons of concrete and the jarring traffice is suspended. Further, there was the resisting strength in that structure to stand under the gales of wind which sweep up and down our Hudson Valley. Further still, there was the accurately calculated force to undergo the

changes of temperature which contract and expand
the steel from midnight to noon, from the torrid
heat of summer up to 120 degrees Fahrenheit on a
July afternoon down to 15 degrees below zero in
the small hours of a February morning. That bridge
spoke of power to achieve and power to sustain.

Christians must possess both varieties of energy.
They must be everlastingly at the work for the
commonweal which God appoints them; and they
must bear the weights of fellow-mortals who jar on
them, the pressures of the winds of current thought
which sweep upon them, and the subtle changes in
climate to which they are exposed every twenty-
four hours and every year of their lives.

That bridge with its traffic illustrates both types
of men and women in the eleventh chapter of
Hebrews:

"who through faith subdued kingdoms, wrought
righteousness, obtained promises . . . turned to
flight the armies of aliens."

No lack of dynamic energy in these believers!

"Others were tortured, not accepting deliverance;
and others had trial of cruel mockings and scourg-
ings, yea, moreover of bonds and imprisonment."

There is static energy. Present-day Christians have
to take it and take it and take it again. And both

types of force result from confident fellowship with God in Christ. They come about "through faith."

Still another characteristic of our day, a characteristic spoken of *ad nauseam*, is *confusion*. Noel Coward writes:

> "In this strange illusion, chaos and confusion,
>   People seem to lose thir way;
> What is there to strive for, love or keep
>   alive for?
> Say, Hey! Hey! call it a day."

But such confusion is no new thing. Holbrook Jackson wrote of the 1890's, the epoch when I was a student at college and seminary:

> "Everybody, mentally and emotionally, was running about in a hundred different directions."

A generation still earlier, Clough declared:

> "Neither battle I see, nor arraying, nor king
>   in Israel;
> Only infinite jumble and mess and
>   dislocation."

What is God's word in the Bible about confusion? To begin with, it suggests that of itself it is hazardous. Here is a text from an ancient battlefield:

> "The forest devoured more people that day than the sword devoured." (2 Sam. 18:8.)

Many more are lost to the Christian forces through moral bewilderment than through hostile factors—theological or ideological.

Again, the Bible makes plain that some confusion is part of spiritual growth. Recall the detail in Isaiah's vision: "and the house was filled with smoke." We do not at once clearly behold the King, high and lifted up. In our Lord's opening of blind eyes, there was a stage when the man saw "men as trees walking." He was on the way to fully restored vision. That is a comforting word for many whose religious sight is still blurred.

Yet again, confusion drives those with even rudimentary faith to God. You recall the scene in the 107th Psalm where the passengers and sailors on that clumsy vessel

> "mount up to the heaven,
> They go down again to the depths:
> Their soul is melted because of trouble.
> They reel to and fro, and stagger like a
>   drunken man,
> And are at their wit's end . . .
> Then . . .

God takes us to our wits' end fairly often in order to induce us to "cry unto Him." Wits' end is a favorable place for religion, and we may congratulate ourselves that this is the dizzy spot where we and our contemporaries are privileged to live.

Finally, confusion is driving many to authoritarianism in religion. They are disposed to pray with the baffled prodigal in the far country:

"Make me as one of thy hired servants."

In economics, individualism is being discarded for collective planning, and much can be said for at least some of it. In religion, Fundamentalism, Roman Catholicism, and other authoritarian movements within communions are seemingly popular. It is not astonishing that ex-Communists become Romanists —both systems are totalitarian. In every city one can discover groups of Protestants moving backward from the liberal point of view to obscurantist positions. They prefer to be "hired servants," not "friends," and to be specifically told rather than to think out for themselves the will of God. But have you noticed in our Lord's parable that while in the far country the prodigal proposed to say this to his father, when he actually stood face to face with him, he omitted it? He could see in his father's face that he wished a *son*, not a hired servant. Free sonship has its dangers. The prodigal knew that well. Today many Protestants are afraid of "the liberty with which Christ makes us free." Nonetheless we are "called for freedom." God desires reliant sons and daughters who think for themselves with the mind of Christ. A servile Church of traditionalists is not the company of the Spirit His heart craves. He wishes those who call no man father upon earth, and refuse to be docile children to any man, but who have direct relations of their own with the invisible and let no human being govern their consciences. That is a thought-provoking text: "Make me as one of thy hired servants."

We have brought forward these various passages of Scripture to illustrate how the Biblical material lends itself to current needs and brings God personally to meet them. The at-present popular Form-Criticism of the Gospels stresses the fact that their stories and conversations were employed in missionary preaching and in sermons in assemblies for worship before they were set down as parts of Gospels. The material has been gone over again and again by speakers seeking to afford the living God in Christ access to men. How its questions challenge: "Why could we not cast it out?" "Why troublest thou the Master any further?" Or the Master's own strained question under a seemingly resultless ministry: "O faithless generation, how long shall I be with you? How long shall I bear with you?" and to Philip: "Have I been so long time with you, and yet . . .?" In its literary form, the Bible for the most part is already a monstrance, holding up God for men's adoration and self-commitment.

There is no substitute for Biblical preaching, not only because of the danger of departing from the

Gospel given once for all in the Self-revelation of God in those books which the Church of many centuries has conserved, attested and transmitted to us; but also because through this literature God comes and meets His people, and is potently felt and known. A sketchy, superficial knowledge of the Bible is crippling to a preacher. By all means let him know his own period—its moods, its trends, its reactions to the epoch in which it finds itself. By all means let him know what is in man, and how human nature, normal and abnormal, responds to the stimuli which impinge upon it. But even more let him know the Word of God historically given in the Scriptures. It is that Word which has brought the Church into being, that Word which has sustained her through the centuries, that Word which in preaching, teaching and sacrament has mediated God's enlightening and empowering presence. Whatever a sermon may lack in literary skill, in eloquence, or in range or depth of spiritual experience, let it be a word of God—a word He Himself speaks of Himself to His children claiming them for His own. This is sacramental preaching, rendering human speech a means of grace through which none less than the Most High God reveals Himself to His sons and daughters.

2

IN THE DEMONSTRATION OF
THE SPIRIT AND OF POWER

*W*RITING TO the Church at Corinth the apostle says that his preaching in that city had been "in demonstration of the Spirit and of power." The word he employs (*apodeixis*) was in technical use among the Stoics for proof drawn from observable facts. Here is the major discouragement of many a hard-working minister who week after week puts study, thought, painstaking writing, and sincere prayer into the composition of his sermons. What comes of it all? It is the seeming futility of his preaching which takes the heart out of many a conscientious ambassador of Christ. What difference is it making? Latimer, in a sermon before King Edward, bursts out:

"Let the preacher preach till his tongue is worn to the stump, nothing is amended."

This resultlessness leads not a few to abandon the ministry. They see their friends and acquaintances in various businesses and professions achieving measurable gains; but how intangible at best are effects from preaching! It seem that very few ever know whether anything which they have said has had spiritual consequences. Canon Twells, the writer of the beautiful hymn "At Even Ere the Sun Was Set," tells in the formal language of devout Victorians:

"A friend of mine, a layman, was in the company of an eminent preacher, then in the decline of life. My friend happened to remark what a comfort it must be to think of all the good he had done by his gift of eloquence. The eyes of the old man filled with tears: 'You little know. You little know!' If I ever turned one heart from the ways of disobedience to the wisdom of the just, God has withheld the assurance from me. I have been admired and run after and flattered; but how gladly would I forget all that, to be told of one single soul I have been instrumental in saving! The eminent preacher entered into his rest," Twells continues. "There was a great funeral. Many passed around the grave who had often hung upon his lips. My friend was there, and by his side was a stranger who was so deeply moved that when all was over my friend said to

him: 'You knew him, I suppose.' 'Knew him? No.
I never spoke to him; but I owe to him my soul.' "

(*Colloquies on Preaching*, by Henry Twells,
1889.)

The Reformed Theology is explicit that both the
Sacraments and the preaching of the Word become
"effectual unto salvation only by the blessing of
Christ and the working of His Spirit in them that
by faith receive them." The Office of Holy Communion in the *Book of Common Prayer* has in its
Prayer of Consecration an Invocation of the Holy
Spirit. Obviously it is not in *man's* power to command the Spirit or to discern clearly His always
mysterious working in a human heart and life. A
minister's concern is to yield himself with all his
capacities as an instrument of the Spirit.

May I adduce an instance from the Scottish pulpit from the time which immediately succeeded the
epoch of Knox? Among the Edinburgh preachers
was one with the name of the earlier national hero,
Robert Bruce. Coming from a ministers' meeting
at which Bruce had been the speaker, one of those
present said:

"O what a strange man is this, for he seemed to
knock down the Spirit of God upon us all,"

alluding to a gesture of his hands on the table at
which he was standing. Bruce impressed contem-

poraries by his resolve to keep himself aware of the presence of God. A frequent hearer of his in Edinburgh speaks of his pausing in silence after standing up in the pulpit before announcing his text, as though saying: "I think it is a great matter to believe that there is a God." Another recounts an incident of his ministry at Larbert on Loch Lomond:

"There was a chamber near by the kirk where he used to go in betwixt sermons" (The two Sunday services were separated by a brief interval during which the parishioners ate a lunch on the gravestones in the kirkyard). "One day some noblemen and gentlemen, who had been hearing him, wearied betwixt sermons, when he stayed longer than he used. They called for the bellman, and desired him to go to him in the little room, and to knock softly at the door, and if he opened to acquaint him that they desired he might begin as soon as conveniently he could, because some of them had far to ride. The bellman did as he was commanded, but Mr. Bruce was so taken up in prayer that he did not hear him. However, the bellman while at the door heard some of Mr. Bruce's words, and came back to those that sent him, and told them that he did not know when the minister would come out. He believed there was somebody with him, for he heard him many times say, with the greatest seriousness, 'That he would not,—he could not go,—unless He came with him, and that he would not go alone'; adding that he never heard the other answer him a word."

The narrative concludes with a statement which contrives with Scot's reserve to say so vastly much:

"When he came out in a little, he was singularly assisted and that afternoon was remarkably useful to many."
(*Bruce's Sermons and Life*, R. Woodrow, Edinburgh, 1843)

Bruce offered a genuine *Epiclesis* upon the preaching of the Word, and there ensued a demonstration of the Spirit and of power.

It is the lack of this effective power in our preaching which makes us look back wistfully to days when sermons had prodigious results. George Borrow in *Lavengro* pictures a crowd of rough men and women on a heath in northern England,

"laborers and mechanics and their wives and children, dusty people, unwashed people, people of no account,"

listening with strained faces to an evangelist speaking from a wagon. How many of us here would have known how to begin or what to say under such conditions? But so potent was the effect of such preaching that the face of England was changed. The definition of religion given by Henry Scougall, that caught the mind of John Wesley:

"the life of God in the soul of man" became fact with thousands previously outside any religious influence. The Divine was patently alive and active in them.

Perhaps the most serious lack of the Church today, as was said in the last chapter, is this awareness of the invading God, and the incalculable results of His indwelling in Christian men and women. In the New Testament there are three striking verbs used of men's treatment of the Spirit of God. Stephen's defence before the throng in Jerusalem concludes: "Ye do always *resist* the Holy Spirit." Most preachers and their people are unaware of any Divine force pressing in upon them. A preacher must unmask the factors constraining men—in their memories, their aspirations, their experiences of failure and success, their obligations—and show how they are opposing the eager Spirit by their indifference, their obtuseness, their preoccupation with a host of interests. The sunlight may be streaming down upon our earth, and our room may be dark because we fail to raise the shade. God is never obtrusive. There must be an invitation: "Ask, and ye shall receive." The tragedy of nations and of individuals is the excluded God.

A second verb is in the Epistle to the Ephesians:

"*Grieve* not the Holy Spirit of God . . . *Let* all bitterness, and wrath, and anger, and clamor, and

evil speaking, *be put away from you*, with all
malice: and be ye kind one to another."

The verb is a passive imperative. It reads not "put
away," which is the burden of so much of our
preaching, but "let them be put away" by the Spirit
of God.

When Messrs. Moody and Sankey were sweeping
Britain some eighty years ago, the average respectable Englishman was repelled by their insistence
that he could not do anything significant to save
himself. *Punch* put this feeling in its jingle:

"Declare not, O Moody, that doing is damning;
    And sing not, O Sankey, that working is sin;
For if piety be not emotional shamming,
    Old duty's bedrock is the place to begin."

But preaching on duty has not produced Christians.
De Quincey describes a preacher

"Who understood by religion simply a respectable
code of ethics—leaning for support upon some great
mysteries dimly traced in the background, and
commemorated in certain great church festivals—"

a pathetically accurate summary of much of what
is heard from our American pulpits today. A vague
God in the background is no present help in ridding

men and communities of most real and aggressive evils. De Quincey goes on:

"It was impossible for any man starting from the low ground of themes so unimpassioned and so desultory as the benefits of industry, the danger from bad companions, the importance of setting a good example, or the value of perseverance—to pump up any persistent steam of earnestness in himself or in his hearers."

And the same may be said for starting from the low ground of our inner life, as psychiatrists unveil it for us, with its frustrations, fears, worries, and the rest, particularly when their origins are traced back to our childhood and blamed on parents or family conditions, or school circumstances, to "pump up" or otherwise become possessed of a "persistent steam of earnestness." But what if God be Himself present? And what if He be heart-broken by our ignorance of His comradeship, our distrusting anxieties, our prejudices, our grudges, our asperities? Men may declare, and often proudly, that they cannot help speaking their minds or showing their feelings. They dislike sneaks who cover up. But if the Spirit be given to remove bitterness, wrath, clamor and other sins of that ilk, why hang on to them? Why continue rough and prickly, a problem in personal relations? New York City, so far as it lies on Manhattan Island, is kept reasonably clean by two rivers, into which at the east and the west end of each street a sewer discharges its filth, which is swept down the Bay and out into the Atlantic. The Holy Spirit is ours, corporately and individually, in the Church, in the nation, in our particular community, to achieve a similar "putting away," if we will only *let* Him.

The third verb is in the First Letter to the Thessalonians: "*Quench* not the Spirit." Every New Testament Christian had an inward fire. It had been kindled first at Pentecost. And every one of them was gifted; but the gift had to be exercised; the flame within had to be "stirred up." The Church of today or of any day is never going to fulfil her task while her members beg off on the plea of their incompetencies. We, ministers and people in the Body of Christ, are all living Post-Pentecost. And none dare think himself unendowed with a divine gift. The tragedy is that we can extinguish the inner blaze. "Ye are My witnesses" and provided with spiritual force to bear testimony in life and action and word. But we can keep our mouths shut, or confine our energies to bread-and-butter jobs, or let our characters remain a miscellaneous picture of things earthy and heavenly, and the earthy much more prominent, with the outcome that the Spirit is stifled and smothered. And the Church, which should be ablaze, is cold and dark. Outsiders see no evidence of the indwelling and transforming God.

There is nothing novel in the combination of these verses with their verbs suggestive of the Spirit as an invasive force. One of the early Gospel hymns by P. P. Philips put them together and many a preacher has followed suit. And to preach cogently on the in-pressing, soul-cleansing, upsurging Spirit, the speaker must himself be an instrument of the Divine. Do you recall a vigorous Hebrew metaphor in one of the early stories in the Book of Judges where it is said:

"The Spirit of the Lord clothed himself with Gideon, and he blew a trumpet,"

and raised the Israelitish clans against Midian? The personality of the man became the vesture of the present Deity. Gideon was Divine might embodied and operating, and himself the convincing witness of God's presence in power among His people.

In Newman's correspondence, a friend writes of the impression Hurrell Froude had made upon him:

"Certainly he has a way of speaking which carries conviction in a very extraordinary way, over and above the arguments he uses."

There is "truth through personality" deriving warmth and cogency from the man with whom truth has clothed itself. It is a well-known fact that creative spirits—artists, novelists, poets, architects, pioneering scientists—are aware of being taken possession of by a mightier than themselves. Their work is their own *plus*, and in the *plus* is its supreme power. The late Gamaliel Bradford, speaking of his own writing, tells us:

"It is the testimony of all who have made great art, and have at all analyzed the process of making it, that something enters in and possesses them far more than mere superficial consciousness or effort. You sit down to your task quite hopeless, discouraged, incapable. Then suddenly, from you know not where, out of the depths of the subconscious, out of the inherited memory of the ages, the power comes upon you, and you speak, or appear to speak, with tongues of angels." (*Life and I*, Houghton Mifflin, 1928.)

It is not that a sermon-writer must sit and wait for this afflatus. Sunday arrives once every seven days whether the afflatus has come or been withheld; but the conscientious workman, toiling with as much brain, heart and literary skill as he can command, is laid hold of and becomes the clothing of the flaming Spirit. He writes better than he knows. Nor can he foretell when the hour of visitation will arrive. It may not be at his desk. Professor H. H. Farmer confessed:

"I have come to have great faith in changes made as it were with one foot already on the pulpit steps"

as the man comes face to face with the people and is keenly aware that through his message God is confronting the congregation. And who of us has not been laid hold on in the very act of preaching and constrained to alter what he had prepared? This is not to validate our chance utterances—sometimes extraordinarily imprudent and even silly —by ascribing them to immediate inspiration. But the entire process of thinking out, writing and re-writing, getting the matter and language in mind, and then delivering it, is all a creative act in which the Spirit may come upon us. To be sure we may not be aware of it. Who has not discovered that when he was least satisfied with a sermon, when he went up into the pulpit disgusted with his meagre mind and clumsy style, or when something at the last moment put him off and robbed him of the enthusiasm which had been his all week, then it was that something in his poor sermon struck fire in a listener? And who also has not had the depressing experience of going to the pulpit in high heart, confident that he had been given a message and had worked it out and up with unusual efficacy only to find that it did not "come off"? "The wind bloweth where it listeth"; so the Spirit. Sometimes He clothes Himself with us, and sometimes we remain a mere bundle of limp garments with no potent Divine presence alive in them. When that disaster happens, we are not necessarily castaways. Years convince us of the correctness of the reply given to the apostle:

"Where there is weakness, My power is shown the more completely." (J. B. Phillips' tr. in *Letters to Young Churches.*)

This is but an instance of a basic truth we have to learn—that in religion there is only one Actor, the living God. We sometimes speak of heroes of the Bible; in fact the entire Biblical literature has a single Hero. A variety of interesting and colorful men and women walk across its pages, but everything of lasting significance is done by God alone. It is a library of "the mighty acts of God." The Germans use the word *Heilsgeschichte* for the whole narrative, "salvation-history." There is only one Saviour. If we would have what occurs in our parish an episode in that sacred story, we must acquire for ourselves a capacity, come by very hardly by active Americans, to "wait upon the Lord." There is a description applied to God in the sublime prayer in the sixty-fourth chapter of Isaiah—a description given in almost breathless astonishment—"From of old men have not heard, nor perceived by the ear, neither hath the eye seen, a God beside thee which worketh for him that waiteth for him." It is almost a complete reversal of the religious outlook of this country for almost a century. We have thought of God as a faithful Helper of those who work for Him. The initiative, the effort, the planning and the performance, has been considered man's. God supplemented, and brought to completion. This prayer stresses God working and man waiting for Him. This is certainly so of the Spirit's role in our sermons. We wait—in prayer, in study, in reverent attempt to frame thought and speech worthy of Him; and He worketh exceeding abundantly above all that we ask or think. The Spirit clothes Himself with a miscellaneous company of preachers, and through them or despite them the Church is served.

Some of us find it difficult to keep aware of the inspiring Spirit of God because we must trudge through a daily routine—study, writing, answering the phone, visiting, attending meetings, etc. Have you ever preached on "He must needs go through Samaria"? Samaria was a district in which our Lord had no special interest, but geographically it lay between Judea and Galilee. It stands for routine—that through which we must needs pass. He found four wells in Samaria: first, the historic Jacob's well—symbol of traditional sources of refreshment available in wearying stretches; second, the Samaritan woman who furnished an occasion of opening up living water; third, her neighbors in Sychar who came trooping to see this penetrating Teacher; and fourth, unknown to Him, the origin in His thought of the parable of the Good Samaritan. Veteran readers will agree that when we plod faithfully through our routine, similar wells disclose themselves and convince us that the Spirit of God is at work, paralleling our prosaic labors.

Speaking of his own preaching and that of his fellow-missionaries, Paul tells us repeatedly that he had been *entrusted with* the Gospel. He was not an originator, but a transmitter. It is this which saves ministers from the seeming immodesty of standing up and telling their fellow-men what they should think and what they should be and do. Browning described his preacher as one "who flashed God's message back to men." To be sure it is not as simple and as external as that. Ezekiel puts his experience of receiving the Word of God for transmission in a vivid picture:

"Son of man, open thy mouth, and eat that I give thee. And when I looked, behold, an hand was sent unto me; and, lo, a roll of a book was therein; and He spread it before me; and it was written within and without. . . . Moreover He said unto me, Son of man, eat that thou findest; eat this roll, and go speak unto the house of Israel."

There is a process of assimilation. The roll contained so much that it was written within and without. What a portrayal of the bewildering miscellaneous impressions which come to us of God's mind towards the welter of human occurrences! We have to assort these impressions, digest them, and when they have become part of ourselves—our conscience, our heart, our mind—speak them, but always as not our own but *given* us.

This sense of the Gospel as entrusted renders us scrupulous in seeing to it that it is the authentic Gospel that we preach. The Gospel was given historically in an event—the life, death, resurrection, return in the Spirit and continuing presence in the Church of Jesus Christ. One may simply think of Him, and ask whether what one is saying accords with His mind.

Again, to recall that the Gospel is a trust prevents us from permitting ourselves—our current opinions, our moods, our preferences and prejudices—to intrude into sermons. "We preach not ourselves." The Gospel has to be personalized through us, and inevitably is colored in the process; but it remains above us and judges us. Even while we phrase and proclaim it, it keeps us its humble servants. James Denney said acutely:

"No man can give at once the impressions that he himself is clever and that Christ is mighty to save."

We were speaking of a serious lack in the experiences of Christians today. There is another such crippling deficiency—contemporary defeatism. It is hard for us oldsters to recapture for you the well-nigh incredible optimism in which our generation was reared. As a schoolboy I recall some lines in one of our readers which we memorized:

> "Though beaten back in many a fray,
> Fresh zeal our hearts will borrow;
> And where the vanguard halts today
> The rear shall camp tomorrow."

That picture of a steadily advancing column was stamped on the walls of our minds. The deity of the western world, that on which it relied confidently, was progress. The complimentary epithet of the day was "forward-looking." It never occurred to anyone that the look ahead might be frightening. The last fifty years have been terribly disillusioning, and a large body of our people have not yet adjusted themselves to the world we now confront. To be sure there was nothing Christian in this trust in an improving world. It has no basis whatsoever in the Bible. It looks forward often to catastrophe, and then to God's redemption. Its typical utterance in this matter is:

> "The Lord is my portion, saith my soul;
> Therefore will I hope in Him."

History in both Testaments was usually harrowing. Believers averted their eyes from it and looked up. Their satisfying expectation was from God.

We are, therefore, in much better position to understand "the hope of the Gospel." And we must make it clear and compelling. Clement of Alexandria spoke of hope as the life-blood of faith:

"When hope expires, it is as if the blood flowed forth and the vitality of faith is destroyed."

Of how many in our congregations, and perhaps among ourselves, is this the reason for our anemic Christianity?

What is this hope born of the Gospel?

(1) Under its God life has purpose and meaning. In his translation of the *Letter to Diognetus* Bishop Lightfoot renders a description of the faith given by this anonymous author to his friend:

"This new interest (*epitédeuma*) which has entered into men's lives now and not before."

Historians write of the "loss of nerve" in the first and second centuries. Against that background Lecky said of the early Church:

"There sprang a stern, aggressive, and at the same time disciplined enthusiasm wholly unlike any other that had been witnessed upon earth." (*History of European Morals*, I:414.)

It is always so where the Gospel grips men. A century ago the young Prince Bismarck, who had given up his inherited Lutheranism under the impact of Strauss and Bauer, was laid hold of by a warm evangelicalism. He wrote his wife:

"I cannot conceive how a man who reflects and yet knows nothing of God, and will know nothing, can endure his life for contempt and boredom. I do not know how I formerly endured. . . . I cannot think why I should not put life aside like a dirty shirt." (*Bismarck*, by C. Grant Robertson, p. 55, London: 1918.)

How rarely today a minister is called to an enthusiastic congregation, so that his task is mainly to organize its zeal! Heartiness has fallen out of fashion, or rather our times lack the conditions which create it. The Gospel has to fetch it from God and set hearts ablaze.

(2) A second assurance is that through Christ men and communities can be *changed*. Early Christian writers are full of this. To quote Clement again:

"Behold the might of the new song! It has made men out of stones, men out of beasts."

In all congregations are men and women who do not expect to become different, and whose acquaintance do not think they will. This is depressing for their pastor and should be disheartening to them. Granted that they are not scandalous evil-doers. No one would list them as exhibits of the grace of God. Their faith lacks anticipation of growth in holiness or in usefulness; and as for our communities, most of their citizens deem them fixed in character: "That's Chicago for you. That's New York," or some much smaller rural or suburban neighborhood. At times we shudder at the completeness of the transformation wrought by anti-Christian ideologies. How swiftly Marxism has remade "holy Russia"! How thoroughly Nazism impregnated eager young Germans! You recall the dictum of Benjamin Kidd:

"There is not an existing institution in the world of civilized humanity which cannot be profoundly modified or altered or abolished in a generation."

But the altering and abolishing are not being done by the Gospel but by its antagonists. Here is the challenge: Can we set forth the Gospel so that God's Spirit through our preaching changes men radically? Do we preach for conversions (to employ that outworn word), to create new consciences, new minds towards God and man? Wingfield-Stratford, in his *History of British Civilization,* speaks of the Christian Church in its more vital impacts upon the nation—in the coming of Augustine of Canterbury, in the Cluniac revival, in the Reformation, in the Wesleyan renewal of evangelical religion—as "a mind-forming society." She shaped the outlooks and molded the purposes of men and women. That is the function of the Gospel. We may not see ourselves confronting with Clement those who are stones or beasts (although unhappily no town is without them), but we face the mixed components of human nature in those we serve and have no doubt that of them all Christ can create sons and daughters of the living God. This is "the hope of the Gospel."

(3) We confidently look for the continuing life of the Church with God. "The gates of hell shall not prevail against it." A people in covenant with God is essential for His purpose. They may be fewer or more numerous, more and less loyal, apparently vigorous or in decline; but they persist. The Church is a basic conviction of the Christian creed and an essential of the Gospel. "The Holy Catholic Church" is as fundamental as "the forgiveness of sins." This does not imply that particular ends which the Church attempts to serve—plans for peace and justice, missionary enterprises, etc.—are

destined to come to pass. It is not that (as many say) "they are too good to be true." Since they are man-made, they contain man's folly and sin. They may not yet be good enough to be true in God's fulfilment, and for the time being they suffer set-backs and sometimes complete annihilation. But if they are aligned with God's will, they are never wholly in vain "in the Lord."

Lord Ashley in 1844, when his bill for the limitation of the hours of labor in factories to ten a day was beaten in the House of Commons, went home and entered in his diary next morning:

"Last night defeated—utterly, singularly, prodigiously defeated by a majority of 138. 'Cast down but not destroyed.' I feel no abatement of faith, no sinking of hope, no relaxation of perseverance. The stillest and darkest hour of the night just precedes the dawn. 'Though it tarry, wait for it,' believing that God sends you a trial, and yet bears you up with a corresponding courage; and, although you may not pass the stream of Jordan it is something that God has permitted you to wash your feet in the waters of the promised land." (*Life of Lord Ashley, Earl of Shaftesbury*, which contains so much of his interesting diary.)

More humane legislation than Lord Ashley glimpsed has come to stand on the statute books. His Christian hope has been justified. But no man's scheme for its realization is without flaw and its defeat and delay may be God's method of purifying it. No plan of ours, however idealistic and apparently Christian, is sure of accomplishment. The one enduring entity is the Body of Christ, the spiritual community in fellowship with God. Its outward forms may change—as indeed they have over the centuries. In some places it may seem to be destroyed, as were the formerly vigorous churches in the Middle East. But a people in covenant with God continues on the earth age after age. They and God's unceasing work in and through them are part of "the hope of the Gospel."

(4) They individually are assured that neither death nor life can separate them from God. The immortality of all souls is no part of the Christian Gospel. There may be many reasons to believe it; but the unique assurance of the Christian faith is that one who has committed himself to Christ in trust and love will never be wrenched from Him by any circumstance or force here or hereafter. J. P. Richter in a vivid essay pictured a mother on her deathbed, grieving not because she is to meet God whom she fears, but to part with God whom she loves.

"One friendship, perfect and divine, had been hers; and now it must end."

She bids farewell to kindred and friends around her bed.

"Now comes that which is the bitterest—I must take farewell of the most Beloved of all, of Thee, my God."

That scene places in sharp focus the essence of the Christian faith. It is a personal relationship with the eternal Father on whose faithfulness in life, in death, and forever, we steadfastly rely. That is the hope of the Gospel.

If we would preach that Gospel accurately, we must go from the vague and hazy notions which float about all our churches and study our New Testament. It throbs with a mighty assurance of God's present energy in the Church. It speaks of "the exceeding greatness of His power to usward who believe," an expression which is rarely on the lips of contemporary Christians. We are aware of the exceeding greatness of His patience with us, of His forgiveness, of His compassion towards us; but not of His power. Something has dropped out of our sight which stood forth clear on their horizon. It furnished the measure of "the exceeding greatness of His power in His people, according to that working of the strength of His might, which He wrought in Christ, when He raised Him from the dead." At Easter we preach upon the resurrection, and often very hesitantly, as though it did not fit into our way of thinking. We sometimes avoid the resurrection altogether, and use the day to commemorate man's endless life, which is only fractionally a Christian conception and largely unrelated with the Gospel. Most of those who crucified Jesus thought He would continue to exist somewhere; but they were resolved to rid their world of Him, for He was a disturbing factor in the Jewish Church and in the Roman Empire. Jesus Himself was not eager for further life in some dim realm of spirits. He had come into this world of His sinning brethren and wished to go on in it lifting them into life with God. It was this, His dearest purpose, which with Himself He had committed to God. A British novelist has said flippantly: "Jesus trusted in God, and God let Him down." But did He?

Resurrection does not mean escape from this tough earth into a more favorable realm. Such a flight would have been for Jesus loss of the battle into which He had thrown His all. Resurrection means return in power, despite death and burial, and going on with divine force in and through His Church, His Body. Easter is the festival of the trustworthiness of God for those who confide in Him.

The New Testament sees Jesus raised from the dead and set at God's right hand "far above all rule and authority and power and dominion, and above every name that is named, not only in this age, but also in that which is to come." The words "rule," "authority," "power," "dominion" have a political connotation; they stand for human society organized to exert force. That was what Jesus encountered in the Jewish Sanhedrin and in the Roman provincial governor. He worsted them and was much more potent *post mortem* than He had been when walking and teaching in their synagogues and temple and up and down the countryside. This is the supreme instance of God's control and mastery of an historic situation. It is such a situation that His Church is blocked by today. It is the rule, authority, power, dominion of hostile ideologies and of frustrating secularism in the minds of men. Here is the current conflict and here is "the exceeding greatness of His power" manifest in that reversal of history which transformed a dead Master into a living Lord for the first Christians. It may be impossible for us to combine the New Testament accounts of what occurred at Joseph's sepulchre and immediately thereafter into a coherent narrative. When a startling event takes place, rarely do all the descriptions of it agree in detail. But the undoubted fact remains that Jesus was more potently alive after His cross and burial than He had been before His arrest. The Christian Church which He sent on its way in conquering might is itself the convincing evidence.

Indeed, it is only for this believing community that He is alive. Surprise is sometimes expressed that there were no appearances to the Sanhedrin, to Pontius Pilate, to the crowds who had stood staring at the place of execution. What dramatic scenes these would have been! But Jesus had no confidence in the merely startling. "If they believe not Moses and the prophets," if righteousness and mercy have no cogent appeal, "neither will they be persuaded though one rose from the dead." The startling may make men gasp for a moment, and send them off chattering of what they have seen, but the effect wears off, and they continue the same shallow, selfish men they have always been. To the priests, to Pilate, to the crowds, Jesus remained dead and buried. They knew and felt nothing of the power of His resurrection. But to Mary Magdalene, to the two whom He joined on the road to Emmaus, to the disciples before whom He stood in the Upper Room, to the five hundred on a mountain in Galilee, to Saul on the Damascus Road, He was compellingly alive and He was empowering. And they, and a growing company infected with their faith, began turning the world upside down. He became "Head over all things to the Church" which now was His Body in and through which He worked on and is working on until this hour. This is "the exceeding greatness of His power to usward who believe." It is of this that every Christian must be a witness.

The resurrection of Christ is the supreme instance
of God's mighty working in human affairs. It is the
convincing instance of His control of history. And
it is in history that our generation most needs to be
assured of His mastering presence. To preach the
resurrection on one Sunday a year only is certainly
to be out of line with the emphasis of the New
Testament. Every Lord's day is a commemoration
of this mighty act of God. It is a living Lord, the
conqueror of death, the Overcomer of the world,
who meets us at His Table, who speaks to us face
to face in His Gospel, who bids us "Be of good
cheer" and shares with us the exceeding greatness
of God's power. This is the indispensable Gospel
for our depressed and often defeatist time. Its plain-
spoken proclamation gives the likeliest opportunity
for a demonstration of the Spirit and of power. The
resurrection is surely not "a great mystery" in De
Quincey's phrase, to be left "dimly traced in the
background." It must stand in the forefront of our
thinking and of our preaching and be at the centre
of the Church's life and work. If in our preaching
we hold up the "monstrance of the Gospel," let us
make sure that it unmistakably displays the victorious Christ, fully adequate to cope with and subdue
all rule, authority, power and dominion, the heart-
ening Leader God has provided for recurring periods
in human history when men's spirits fail them, and
their horizon is dark with anxiety and fear. The

sovereignty of God over the bewildering course of affairs is the conviction which the Church of today requires. Its evidence is given most strikingly in the resurrection of Jesus. Are we convinced of it? Are our people convinced of it?

You may recall an experience in which an outstanding preacher of the second half of the nineteenth century was laid hold of by this fact. Dr. R. W. Dale of Birmingham, a massive theological thinker and a glowing speaker, was writing an Easter sermon. When he was half-way through, the thought of the risen Lord, he tells us, broke in upon him as it had never done before.

" 'Christ is alive,' I said to myself, 'alive!' and then I paused; 'alive!' and then I paused again: 'alive!' Can that be really true? living as really as I myself am? I got up and walked about repeating: 'Christ is living! Christ is living!' At first it seemed strange and hardly true, but at last it came upon me as a burst of sudden glory; yes, Christ is living. It was to me a new discovery. I thought that all along I had believed it; but not until that moment did I feel sure of it. I then said: 'My people shall know it; I shall preach about it again and again until they believe it as I do now.'" (*Life of R. W. Dale*, by A.W.W. Dale, pp. 642, 643, New York: 1899.)

The morning service at Carr's Lane thereafter had in it an Easter hymn, no matter what the season.

And Dr. Dale put this new-found conviction to practical effect in his book, *The Living Christ and the Four Gospels*—a stabilizing influence in my student days a half century and more ago amid the critical discussions over the historicity of the Gospel narratives.

That is not our current difficulty; but something much more immediately terrifying and disheartening—the appalling world scene and the consequent depressed condition of mind among Christians. The fact of the resurrection of Jesus Christ and its indisputable testimony to the working of God in events with exceeding great might through His Church, the Body of the living Christ, is the message which God is putting on the lips of preachers for such a time as this.

As in the first generation of Christians Jesus remains dead and buried for the great mass of men. There is no point of contact in their spirits which He can touch and to which He can manifest Himself. But now, as then, alive to and in His Church, He through its witness, may set them questioning, render them wistful, draw them into the fellowship of believing disciples, and disclose Himself to them in power.

There is a subtle temptation for ministers in preaching upon such basic convictions of the Gospel as we have been mentioning—the temptation of unreality, of speaking familiarly of experiences to

which we are strangers. Because we talk of "the
hope of the Gospel" or of "the exceeding greatness
of God's power to usward" there is no reason for
thinking that we know them. There is point in the
old spiritual: "Were You There When They Crucified My Lord?" Were you *there*? A recent poet
has put this strikingly in a sonnet entitled *The
Travel Bureau*:

All day she sits behind a bright brass rail
Planning proud journeyings in words that bring
Far places near—high-colored words that sing—
'The Taj Mahal at Agra' . . . 'Kashmir's Vale' . . .
Spanning wide spaces with her clear detail,
'Seville or Fiesole in spring,'—
'Through the fjords in June'—her words take wing:
She is the minstrel of the great Out-trail!

At half-past five she puts her maps away,
Puts on a grey meek hat, and braves the sleet,
A timid eye on traffic. Dully grey
The house that harbors her in a grey street,
The close, sequestered, colorless retreat,
Where she was born; where she will always stay.

3

A LIVING SACRIFICE YOUR
REASONABLE WORSHIP

*T*HE AIM of every sermon is to induce
commitment of listeners to God for the achievement of His purpose in their lives and in their
world. It must accomplish the self-offering of the
prayer in the Communion Service, which reaches a
climax in the words:

"And here we offer and present unto thee, O
Lord, our selves, our souls and bodies, to be a reasonable, holy, and living sacrifice unto thee."

To bring such commitment to pass, a sermon
must have pointedness. Baxter, in counselling the
preachers of his time, gave them the rule: *Generalia
non pungunt*, which we may render, Generalities
do not puncture. Most sermons fail because the

preacher has not made plain to himself precisely what he is seeking to press these men and women before him to be and to do. Is there anything more ineffective than the glib statements: "Use Christ's way in human relations"; "Let His Spirit control our country's foreign policy"; "Embody His love in our economic and industrial practices." Have you come across some lines of W. H. Auden, which preachers may well take to heart:

> ". . . pawed-at and gossiped-over
> By the promiscuous crowd,
>
> .   .   .   .
>
> All words like peace and love,
> All sane affirmative speech,
> Had been soiled, profaned, debased
> To a horrid mechanical screech." *

A major fault of present preaching, particularly on social themes, is that sermons cover too wide a stretch of territory and end by saying nothing sufficiently concrete to guide people to any specified endeavor. There is nothing in them to which objection can be taken, and equally nothing which lays hold of anyone's conscience as an obligation. It is such meaningless and purposeless preaching which bores congregations.

* From the poem "To Reinhold and Ursula Niebuhr" in *Nones* published by Random House, Inc. Used by permission.

This is not a plea for exhortations to Christian duty. The Gospel is never a summons to human endeavor. It is a setting forth of God in Christ. Recall the order of topics in that Communion Prayer. It begins with a thanksgiving for God's manifestation of Himself in His redeeming Son:

"having in remembrance his blessed passion and precious death, his mighty resurrection and glorious ascension" and "the innumerable benefits procured unto us by the same."

With all this before them, inevitably thoughtful communicants are moved to say: "And here we offer and present unto thee, O Lord." There is no monstrance of the Gospel whatsoever in a ringing call to do this or that, however specifically set forth. The apostle, in the letter to the Ephesians, became very specific in his outlines of Christian duty for parents and children, for masters and slaves; for the converted thief. But it is only after he has set them "in heavenly places" with God's eternal purpose before their eyes and the unsearchable riches of His grace in Christ moving them. That is the only climate in which Christian duty becomes clear and possible. The curse of our pulpit is its bald moralism. The ambassador of Christ forgets his embassy, says next to nothing of the Master he is representing, and spends his time telling those before him what they ought to be and to do. With the result that little or nothing happens. That way lies futility, a futility that has been demonstrated generation after generation in the history of the Christian Church.

We have passed through an activist epoch in the Church in this country. Movements, crusades, campaigns, missions, have filled the horizon. One sometimes wonders what there has been in public worship for the very large number of persons who were in no position to participate in these strenuous efforts—the aged, the handicapped, those below par in health of body and of mind. Our Lord's gracious invitation to "the weary and heavy laden" has not been prominent in American preaching. They have had to content themselves with what they got from prayers and hymns and the always tender Sacrament of the broken Body and outpoured Blood. In fact, "the weary and heavy laden" form a large proportion in every congregation. A faithful pastor, looking over his people from the pulpit, knows the burdens, the frustrations, the tragedies, which exist in home after home. It is one thing to become fired by a subject and to set it forth brilliantly and cogently; it is something else to see distinctly the minds and hearts of men and women and bring Christ to them in His august majesty and His moving tenderness.

Suffer me to suggest texts and their treatments which have seemed to be useful along this line:

Here is the problem of limitations with which all of us are gallingly tormented. Have you ever noticed the two sides of a hedge in the Book of Job? From the outside we hear Satan scornfully telling the Almighty: "Hast Thou not made a hedge about him?" (1:10) and from the inside the bereaved and suffering patriarch of Uz speaks pitifully of himself as "a man whom God hath hedged in." (3:23.) To be just to the chief message of this profound book, we must point out that hedges are not always as fixed as they seem. The three friends kept insisting on the theological hedge in the conventional explanation of suffering as due to sin. And the honest Job would have none of it and fought his way out, not into a more reasonable interpretation of suffering, for the book offers none, but into an ampler and closer fellowship with God: "I had heard of Thee by the hearing of the ear, but now mine eye seeth Thee. Wherefore I abhor myself, and repent in dust and ashes." The torturing hedge that every woe has some sin as its cause is gone. But hedges are planted by God over the entire human landscape and men and nations must live within them. What, then, is their meaning in the mercy of God? We discover it, as this book does, by asking, From what are we hedged out? and To what are we hedged in?

You will recall that even the universally endowed Shakespeare speaks of himself as looking beyond his hedge—"Desiring this man's art and that man's scope." How little he suspected his own peril from which his limitations safeguarded him! "Sir," said Dr. Johnson, "a man may be so much of everything, that he is nothing of anything." When once we realize that on the other side of our hedge is the Satan of diffusion, we learn (with Wordsworth)

"to live
    In reconcilement with our stinted powers."

And more important is to ask, What is God hedging us into? A favorite hymn of the Church today is George Matheson's "O Love That Wilt Not Let Me Go." Not all of us recall that the eloquent preacher who penned those lines was blind. As a student I used to walk down to a very poor district in Edinburgh where he preached in a great barn of a building to a working-class congregation. He had to be led up into the pulpit, and usually he repeated from memory both Scripture lessons and offered exquisitely beautiful prayers, many of which were recorded and appear in his books. When he laid down his charge, he said to his devoted people:

"I came a taper amid the torches (the pulpit lights of the Scottish capital) My place was down in the valley—the Stockbridge Valley. There you will see man outside the stage, with the lights suppressed, and the music silent, and the dancing ceased—man

unconventional, man natural, man struggling hand
to hand with life's poverty and toil. These were the
masses before which I stood—an atom in the crowd.
It was a tragic spectacle; it was blind Samson with
his hands upon the gates of Gaza. The Philistines
laughed; but I think I lifted these gates one inch.
And I think that next to the strength of God, and
next again to your kind cooperation, I am indebted
to my own weakness. These sons of toil said: 'Here
is a man with an environment no less unfavorable
than ours—barred by every gate of fortune, yet re-
fusing to give in—overtaken by the night, yet confident of the morning. . . . My sermons may have
flown over your heads like the bird of Paradise; but
my life has been level with your own—an obstructed
life, a circumscribed life, but a life of boundless
sanguineness." (*Life of G. Matheson*, By D. Mac-
millan, pp. 325–326. A. C. Armstrong & Son:
1907.)

There was a servant of God asking, To what am I
hedged in? and discovering in his blindness God's
assistance to his ministry.

Towards the end of his long and active life General William Booth of the Salvation Army under-
went a serious operation upon his eyes, and it fell
to his son to tell him that the doctors feared he
would not see again. The old man said:

"Bramwell, I have done what I could for God
and for the people with my eyes. Now I shall do

for God and for the people what I can without my eyes."

Through some such simple message one may try to enable restricted folk individually and nationally to present themselves to God a living sacrifice.

In the prayer which Naomi offered for her daughters-in-law there is similar insight into responsibility. The lonely old woman asked:

"The Lord grant that ye may find rest, each of you, in the house of her husband."

What a strange place to expect rest! Most wives ask for a change of scene and relief from the routine of household duties; but Naomi knew the restfulness of obligations. For an unrestful voyage, cross the ocean in a ship without cargo.

This picturesque text with its spiky hedge applies to nations as well as to individuals. For many decades our country like the wealthy man of Uz, enjoyed unique peace and prosperity. Many of our contemporaries are thinking with Job nostalgically:

"Oh that I were as in months past,
    As in the days when God preserved me . . .
    When I washed my steps with butter,
    And the rock poured me out rivers of oil."

But clearly God has hedged us in to the major obligation of restoring a ruined world and lifting up to a decent livelihood many substandard peoples. In this practical sense we can become "fathers to the poor," "eyes to the blind, and feet to the lame." It involves sacrifice of comfort and luxuries and perhaps life in order to "break the jaws" of aggressive enslavers and "pluck the spoil out of their teeth." We hear and shall hear groaning under the load of taxation; but let us not forget the despotic Satan on the other side of the hedge waiting to destroy our, and all men's, hard-won liberties under God and the even more devastating Satan of national irresponsibility who would rob our country of its conscience.

We grumble at times that we are "tied down"— by our work, by our creed, by some small town or confining circle in a city, by a particular church, by a wife or by children. For most of us these ties are our salvation, and without them we should lose our usefulness. Further, they are restful, for there is nothing more exhausting than to live without compelling duties, asking ourselves what to do next to justify our existence or pass our time. Are you familiar with Lowell's charming lines upon his wife:

"I love her with a love as still
    As a broad river's peaceful mill
Which by high tower and lowly mill
Goes wandering at its own sweet will,
    And yet doth ever flow aright."

"And on its full, deep breast serene,
   Like quiet isles, by duties lie;
It flows around them and between,
And makes them fresh, and fair, and green,
   Sweet homes wherein to live and die."

Naomi knew that love brings with it responsibility, and makes responsibility delightful. It is the discovery of Jesus when He bade us "Take My yoke upon you and ye shall find rest unto your souls." He was not ashamed to call men brethren, and in laying down His life for them, He found His satisfaction. It is the rest of God Himself, the Creator who fainteth not, neither is weary—a rest which He shares with us as we enter into His responsibilities, the rest that remaineth for the people of God, when we dwell in the house of the Lord for ever. Here is an offering to God of those at rest in the discharge of their obligations.

A most menacingly irreligious attitude among many in our day is to view God as a possible accessory to our plans. Faith in Him is commended as a therapeutic aid to mental health, or as a dynamic drive towards social betterment. God is not loved for His own sake, but for His utility to us. It is a relapse to a crude form of magic. One is reminded of the story of Micah of Mount Ephraim in the Book of Judges, who induced a traveling Levite to become his private chaplain and provided him with paraphernalia of worship in his house of gods—an ephod, teraphim and an image. The complacent Micah declares that with everything so satisfactorily arranged: "Now know I that the Lord will do me good, seeing I have a Levite to my priest." We have mastered the forces of nature to our uses, why not the forces of the Spirit? In a hundred ways we are attempting it. It is not God who owns and employs us, but we Him. Happily for self-assured Micah, his was a troubled time, and a company of invading Danites came along and despoiled his house of gods and persuaded his chaplain that it was better for him to be priest to a tribe in Israel than to a private individual. We hear Micah bitterly complaining: "Ye have taken away my gods which I made, and the priest, and ye are gone away; and what have I more?" He must learn that he has as much as he ever possessed. The living God remains God, and with these crude idolatrous accessories gone, there is some chance of his being found of Him. Man-made things—credal interpretations, ritual forms, organized institutions, the man-devised addenda—valuable in their time—are shaken and removed, "that those things which cannot be shaken may remain." Micah may now discover the eternal God his dwelling place in all generations; to whom he may present himself a living sacrifice, his reasonable worship.

You and I preach to men and women who have

first-hand experience, many of them, of the appalling brutalities of war. If they are to present themselves to God as trustful believers, they must have some interpretation which satisfies their intelligence of His mysterious and harsh discipline. In the pastoral epistles a strange schoolmaster is suggested. The writer speaks of

"Hymenaeus and Alexander, whom I delivered unto Satan that they might be taught not to blaspheme."

What parents would select such a teacher for their young hopefuls? Hymenaeus and Alexander were not hopefuls but incorrigibles. And think of a Christian apostle confiding even problem pupils to him for education! One remembers Regan's comment on King Lear,

"O sir, to wilful men
    The injuries that they themselves procure
    Must be their schoolmasters."

The Lear who meets us at the climax of the drama is so mellowed and disciplined that Shakespeare reconciles us to his terrible education. A large part of our world has been in a similar devilish schoolroom. It is an education which at best only offers negative results—"that they might be taught *not* to blaspheme." Satanic war may teach us not to be arrogant, nor grasping, nor aggressive. But for nations and for individuals Satan provides a meagre schooling. All that is most worth acquiring has to be learned at the feet of another Master. We are as yet too near the war years, indeed in the midst of them still, to be able to assess the gains in education they have brought us. But here is a New Testament interpretation of grim providences. One sees many individuals submitted to like training. Germany's great hymn-writer Paulus Gerhardt, who lived through the stark Thirty Years' War, whose loved wife and four children were taken from him, who was left with one small child in his home to minister in an uncongenial parish at Lübben, and to whom we owe the lovely evening hymns, "Nun ruhen alle Wälder," "O Haupt voll Blut and Wunden," and "Befiehl du deine Wege" which John Wesley rendered in his "Commit Thou All Thy Griefs," has left to posterity a portrait under which is this inscription: *Theologus in cribro Sathanas versatus.* Next only to Luther, Gerhardt is the most loved hymn-writer of the German Evangelical Churches.

Another approach to this same aspect of our contemporary situation can be made through an Old Testament text—part of the climax of one of the profoundest psalms:

"Make us glad according to the days wherein Thou hast afflicted us, and the years wherein we have seen evil."

Measures are an interesting subject. One marvels at the ingenuity of those who devised them. And how striking it is that in this machine age we still calculate the capacities of our engines in locomotives, motors and airplanes by horsepower! An old nag is trudging along or flying with Pegasus wings in the most recently contrived jet plane. And how calculate the quantum of joy for which we presume to pray? Is there a proportion of some sort between days of gloom and years of gladness?

Readers of Bulwer-Lytton's *Last Days of Pompeii*, (and Bulwer-Lytton still remains one of the most satisfactory of our historical novelists) will recall the blind slave girl Nydia, who moves about the city streets singing her plaintive song:

"Ye have a world of light
　　Where love in the loved rejoices;
But the blind girl's home is the House of Night,
　　And its beings are empty voices.
As one in the realm below,
I stand by the streams of woe.
I hear the vain shadows glide,
I feel their soft breath at my side.
And I thirst the loved forms to see,
　　And I stretch my fond arms around,
　　And I catch but a shapeless sound,
For the living are ghosts to me."

Then comes the fateful day when Vesuvius erupts, and in the pall of smoke and falling ashes the inhabitants rush about in terror, while Nydia, wonted to darkness, treads the streets unerringly, and finds and rescues her beloved. What new perceptions and finer sensitiveness are years in a house of night bringing to our country?

You will recall that it was the fateful decade when England was menaced by the Armada which saw Shakespeare producing his moving utterances of patriotism:

> "This scepter'd isle,
>
> .   .   .   .   .   .
>
> This other Eden, this demiparadise;
> This fortress built by Nature for herself
> Against infection and the hand of war,
>
> .   .   .   .   .   .
>
> This precious stone set in the silver sea,
> Which serves it in the office of a wall
> Or as a moat defensive to a house,
> Against the envy of less happier lands,
> This blessed plot, this earth, this realm,
> this England,
> This land of such dear souls, this dear,
> dear land,
> England, bound in with the triumphant
> sea,
> Whose rocky shore beats back the envious siege. . . ."

Emergencies bring home to us the preciousness of what is ours.

Again you will recall that when Britain blockaded the continent in the Napoleonic wars, chemists, geologists, archaeologists, zoologists, botanists, in France prevented from exploring abroad, worked at home and opened up remarkable riches hitherto ignored. Necessity is a stern mother, but she urges her children forward by mighty strides. Charles Darwin confessed:

"If I had not been so great an invalid, I should not have done nearly so much work."

Ours is a period of baffling questioning. That augurs well for intellectual gains. A nineteenth-century psalmist who addresses God as the "kindly Light amid the encircling gloom" owns of himself:

"It is very painful to be haunted by wandering doubts, to have thoughts shoot across the mind about the reality of religion altogether."

Until we question, our faith is just credulity. Coleridge put it:

"You do not believe; you believe that you believe."

If the mighty psalm from which this text comes were written as a hymn to be sung in the Second Temple, its author has before him the bleak years of the Exile. And it was in them that Israel's richest

literary contributions to mankind were penned.
Prophetic historians collected and edited the stories
of her past; Jeremiah, Ezekiel, Second Isaiah and
other noble prophets gave us their oracles, Job was
composed, and the profoundest psalms added to the
hymnal of the Temple. Who can guess what spiritual wealth is being laid up by tortured mankind,
and especially by sorely puzzled believers in the
Church of Christ, in these years wherein we look
out fearsomely upon evil?

In these sobered days we do well to confront
congregations with the function which tragedy
plays in life. Have you ever thought of Judas
Iscariot as an answer to prayer? St. Luke's narrative reads:

"And it came to pass in those days, that He went
out into a mountain to pray, and continued all night
in prayer to God. And when it was day, He called
unto Him His disciples: and of them He chose
twelve, whom also He named apostles." (Here follow the names of those selected, concluding with)
"and Judas Iscariot, which also was the traitor."

Could men have been more thoughtfully and
devoutly selected? Eleven of them proved variously
capable and steadfast. We must keep our perspec-
tive on God's ordering of human life. There is an
overwhelming balance of good. A generous proportion of those with whom life associates us make us

thankful to Him who gives them to us. But the haunting query persists, Why to the prayer of a dutiful Son did God's response include one who betrayed him?

Our Lord "knew what was in man"; but there is an unpredictable element in life. Perhaps even for God there may be an unforeseeable component in His creation. With the introduction of human freedom into the law-abiding universe His creation contains the risk of tragedy.

Life has many happy surprises. There is a tone of grateful amazement in Jesus' saying to the eleven in the Upper Room: "Ye are they which have continued with Me in My temptations." The unexpected must always be included in our outlooks and it may be tragic. In a letter Keats wrote:

"While we are laughing the seed of some trouble is put into the wide arable land of events—while we are laughing, it sprouts, it grows, and suddenly bears a poisoned fruit which we must pluck."

When our Lord's farmer has sown good seed in his field, an enemy came while he slept and sowed tares. That is life, as Jesus' penetrating eyes interpret it. Even at its loftiest, when shared in prayer with a loving and wise Father, part of the answer is this man of Kerioth.

There is no closing our eyes to the sombre possibilities in all earthly existence. To begin with,

ours is a dangerous planet where hurricanes, earth-
quakes, floods, bacilli, diseases of the body and of
the mind may wreck us. Accidents which overtake
individuals and communities remind us of the un-
anticipated as an essential element in our earthly
education.

We carry possibilities of disaster in ourselves. No
one tempted Judas. He was the architect of his own
doom. If at the last he went out and hanged himself, he had been doing that all along.

> "In tragic life, God wot,
>   No villain need be. Passions spin the plot.
> We are betrayed by what is false within."

Again, as in our Lord's case, fellow-men may be
the cause of our tragedies. The affectionate Desde-
mona and the confiding Othello are victims of the
sinister Iago. What of the woesome millions whom
war drags into wretchedness?

Such tragedies become more poignant still when
brought on by those in whom we ourselves have re-
posed our trust. Jesus expected misunderstanding
in the leaders of the Jewish Church and in Pontius
Pilate. They moved in different worlds. But that
one within His own loyal circle should deliberately
sell Him to His foes!

> "It was not an enemy, then would I hove borne
> it; neither was it he that hated me that did magnify

himself against me. But it was thou, mine acquaintance. We took sweet counsel together, we walked unto the house of God in company."

"Judas, betrayest thou the Son of man with a kiss?" Are there any tragedies comparable to those between friends, above all between lovers? It is in the most intimate and sacred relationships that the bitterest disasters lurk.

Most staggering is it when God is involved. Had our Lord used His own judgment in the choice of apostles, He might have blamed His stupidity. But these names were spread out before the All-wise for an entire night, and Judas was as truly a God-send as Peter or John. Was not the falsity of this traitor one of the factors in the heart-broken cry: "My God, why hast *Thou* forsaken Me?"

God's guidance in the selection of the Twelve remains an insoluble puzzle. But so does much else on our human scene. In the last century, Thomas Erskine wrote:

"Is it not a mystery that God should be omnipotent love, and yet that the world should be just a great cauldron boiling over with violence and pollution and misery?"

It has not changed for the better a hundred years later. But it is *God's* world. We may blame Him for a vast deal which we fancy might and should have been omitted. Why are appalling concomitants mingled with conscientiously wise decisions? Why is the criss-cross of good and evil, the loftiest and the brutallest, so tangled in the web of human affairs? You may recall Thomas Hardy's taunting comment on Tess' devotion to the lover who lured her to a disastrous fate:

"Where was the providence of her simple faith? Perhaps, like that other god of whom the ironical Tishbite spoke, He was talking, or He was pursuing, or He was on a journey, or peradventure He was sleeping and not to be awaked. Why it was that upon this beautiful feminine tissue, sensitive as gossamer and practically blank as snow as yet, there should have been traced such a coarse pattern as it was to receive; why so often the coarse appropriates the finer thus, the wrong man the woman, the wrong woman the man, many thousand years of analytical philosophy have failed to explain to our sense of order."

But what is "our sense of order"? Are we competent to judge the arrangement of this complex scheme of things? When we are baffled by the inclusion of Judas in an answer to prayer, we must take a larger view of our Lord's career, including the cross and subsequent centuries. This traitor was a factor in the appalling and sublime event at Golgotha. Suppose there had been no Calvary, would Jesus have been the Saviour of the world?

In the bitter wars of the seventeenth century, a son of the Duke of Ormonde gallantly laid down his life in what his father and he believed the cause of justice. Someone commiserated the elder man on his sore loss. The Duke replied:

"I would not give my dead son for the best living son in Christendom."

Yes, life is tragic, tragic for man and for Almighty God. The cross has been in it from the foundation of the world. It was through suffering that the Son of man was made mature, and through tragedy that His brethren achieve ends for which generations rise up, and call them blessed. Why this or that particular tragedy is necessary in God's purposes, or why good and evil are mixed in His answers to our prayers, none may presume to say. "His way is in the sea and His paths in the deep waters, and His footsteps are not known." But those who, like His beloved Son, make their choices in prayer, discover themselves led by a way they know not to a destination where they see of the travail of their souls and are satisfied. It is ourselves, wrapped in clouds and darkness, which in this confused existence we offer and present unto God.

The noblest interpretation of God's purpose in tragedy is given in the poem upon the Suffering Servant in Isaiah 52:13—53:12. Preachers would do well to take the entire poem and give its historical meaning in the case of Israel whose resurrection after vicarious self-offering unto death for the sins of many this poet-prophet asserts. Few in our congregations have any idea of the origin of this prophecy. The poem is certainly the most influential ever written. It lighted our Lord's career to its agonized and glorious climax on the cross and beyond through the grave to victory. It furnished the chief point in the theology of the early Church, where apostles preached Christ's death for our sins "according to the Scriptures" and His resurrection "according to the Scriptures," and this is the most explicit Scripture which sets them forth. It was the ideal which the author placed before his people, and there were never enough of them to respond to it and put it to the test. So it waited until He who embodied God's purpose, He in whom all the promises find their Yea, came and uttered His Amen to them in His life, death and triumphant rising.

Indeed, the Servant of the Lord in the exilic Isaiah is a theme well deserving our study and preaching. Have you noticed the utterly different servants this prophet thinks God is employing? There is that victorious Persian sovereign, Cyrus, who topples over proud empire after empire, and is God's agent on the scene of history, His Messiah, he is called in one place, to destroy Babylon and let the captive people go free to return to their homeland and a wider missionary task to the nations. Then there is Israel, God's servant people, or perhaps the responsive spiritual nucleus in Israel whose ears are awake to God's voice. If God were served only by obedient nations, His sovereignty in history would be severely limited, but those who do not even know Him are employed to discharge His purposes. That is a comforting conviction in our world.

"A gracious spirit o'er this earth presides . . .
And tendency benign, directing those
Who care not, know not, think not, what they do."
(Wordsworth, *Prelude*, Bk. V)

But, of course, there is a world of difference between God's use of an unwitting agent, like Cyrus and his Persians, and His comradely employment of His devoutly responsive people, His believing Church. It is our alertness to His hints and suggestions which makes us His friends, and His companionable partners in history. No book brings this out more tellingly than this of Second Isaiah.

It contains a very great text, used twice by Samuel Rutherford in the stormy seventeenth century at a crisis in the Scottish Church: "Fear not, thou worm Jacob." That is the sort of text which catches attention as soon as the preacher announces it. Again and again God's people become defeatist, and act like worms. God does not discard them as hopeless; but they constitute a hard problem. He must lift them to their feet if they are to be His comrades in service. It is that task which this prophet of comfort undertakes. "Fear not," he keeps saying to these timid and apprehensive Jews in Babylon. He hears God assuring them:

"I am thy God: I will strengthen thee; yea, I will help thee; yea, I will uphold thee with My victorious right hand."

If one studies the metaphors the poet employs, one has the promise of a miraculous transformation of the worm Church:

"Behold I will make thee a new sharp threshing instrument having teeth": (What a change from a soft, crawling worm!) "thou shalt thresh the mountains, and make them small, and shalt make the hills as chaff."

That is a function of believers, to possess and express clear-cut convictions which winnow the miscellaneous opinions uttered by the mass of men. Such outspoken utterance of sharp views threshes mountains and hills which obstruct God's purposes. Think of the objections which men conjure up and how towering they frequently seem. But mountains and hills disappear, are chewed up (so to speak) when clear-seeing men of faith state their convictions in words which have edges and points. No worms will ever do that; Christians must become vertebrate, upstanding creatures, boldly frank in the comradeship of their God. No wonder Samuel Rutherford took that text from Isaiah 41 in a discouraging day and commends it by his example to us in a time when many of God's people are once more as worms. Rutherford induced his listeners to get on their feet and stand fast, and they made the Church of their land and age a mighty force. "Fear not, thou worm Jacob."

In uncertain periods there is a desire for security. True religion is a reply to that need. The Psalms are full of epithets for God as defence, "a rock of habitation to which His people may continually resort." The difficulty with most of us is that we do not abide within our defences. In the narrative of those cities provided for the protection of the hunted in ancient Israel, there is a fine text where the hunted who has grown careless is rebuked: "He should have remained in the city of his refuge." (Numb. 35:28.) That merciful provision becomes a beautiful symbol for the refuges we discover in the landscape of life. To begin with there is our home. Folk often stray out of it through sheer thoughtlessness. You may recall that Charles Lamb placed an affectionate inscription on the fly-leaf of a volume of his poems which he presented to his sister. Commenting on it to Coleridge he said:

"It will be unexpected and it will give her pleasure. There is a monotony in the affections, which people living together are not to give in to; a sort of indifference in the expression of kindness for each other, which demands that we should sometimes call to our aid the trickery of surprise."

Another refuge is friendship. Think of the personal greetings with which Paul remembers friends in his letters. "Salute Rufus and his mother *and mine*." How gracious the apostle's recognition of the care of him by an elderly woman! Place beside it what he says of fellow-workers at Colosse, "men that have been a comfort to me." Still another we find in books—"friends on the shelf," Bradford Torrey wrote of them. Edward Rowland Sill speaks of "books of refuge," and Leslie Stephen tells how at the time of his wife's death he found solace in reading Wordsworth. And there is our work—a most certain refuge. Emily Dickinson wrote to a friend:

"I am glad you work. Work is a bleak redeemer, but it does redeem; it tires the flesh so that it cannot tease the spirit."

Again there is the weekly day of rest and worship. "Thou art a port protected from storms that round us rise." Happy they who maintain this refuge in these unrestful times. Yet again there is the Church. Newman entitled a sermon preached in St. Mary's,

Oxford: "The Church the Home of the Lonely." Two charming Japanese who arrived in this country before World War II and found our people generally most hostile told me that the one place where they invariably received a friendly welcome was the Church, so that, although not Christians, they attended every Sunday. Supremely there is Christ Himself. "Other refuge have I none," but we must stick to Him. "Keep yourselves in the love of God" and that is found most tenacious in Christ Jesus our Lord. Only secure selves are whole men to be presented a living sacrifice.

Have you ever noticed how the Bible more than once speaks of the subtle responsiveness of circumstances to the intents of men's minds? Micah puts it strikingly:

"Woe to them that devise iniquity and work evil upon their beds! when the morning is light they practise it, *because it is in the power of their hands.*"

Macbeth's mind is filled with ambition, an impossible ambition:

"To be king stands not within the prospect of belief."

It involves the doing away with Duncan. Macbeth confesses:

"My thought, whose murder yet is but fantastical."

Then Duncan is under his roof, and his wife, urging him on, points out how circumstances have become the confederates of his secret thoughts:

"When you durst do it, nor time nor place
    Did then adhere, and yet you would make
    both:
They have made themselves."

We speak of unanswered prayers; but what of the pathos of some of the answers to prayer? "God gave them their request, but sent leanness into their souls." One encounters these skeletal souls, seemingly starved, because of their own meagre demands on life. And how appalling is the magnetism of the things on which hearts become set:

"Yea, he loved cursing, and it came unto him;
And he delighted not in blessing, and it was far
    from him.
He clothed himself also with cursing, as with his
    garment,
And it came into his inward parts like water,
And like oil into his bones." (Ps. 109: 17–18.)

Happily this magnetism of thoughts work for righteousness too. Many have preached on the women at the tomb:

"And they were saying, Who shall roll us away the stone from the door of the sepulchre? And when they looked, they saw that the stone was rolled away."

Similarly when Peter was being liberated from prison, there was that obstructing iron gate:

"When they were past the first and the second ward, . . . they came unto the iron gate, that leadeth unto the city; which opened to them of his own accord."

How all-important it is that ourselves, with our uncanny correspondences with the universe about us, should be presented sacrifices unto God!

In bringing this chapter to a close, may a veteran in the ministry speak for a few minutes on the drains of a lifework which must be peculiarly personal? Our one tool is just ourselves, and the strains upon it are wearing. Those who arranged for the service of the ancient Levites realised this. A narrative in the Book of Numbers reads:

"Two wagons and four oxen Moses gave unto the sons of Gershon, according to their service; and four wagons and eight oxen he gave unto the sons of Merari, according unto their service, under the hand of Ithamar, the son of Aaron the priest; But unto the sons of Kohath he gave none: because the service of the sanctuary belonging unto them was that they should bear upon their shoulders."

There are many useful tasks which can be performed with various helps. Even in the ministry there are some tasks which permit of these assistances. But those who would minister to their brethren in the inner sanctuaries of their souls have to carry the loads on their own shoulders. It is so in the sanctuary of truth. Those alone who have felt for themselves the acute pain and staggering force of the difficulties of faith are of service to those in doubt. A very saintly ecclesiastic of the last century, at a time when Jowett, the master of Balliol, was regarded with extreme suspicion as a questionable believer, wrote after his wife's death:

"Jowett has been of use to me, because he knows on what foundations our faith rests. Others have been most kind and sympathizing; but cut-and-dry sentiments, in which everything is taken for granted, do me no good at all."

The Russian novelist Dostoievsky tells us in his Journal: "My hosanna has passed through the great purgatory of doubt." Giordano Bruno, burned at the stake for his own honesty of thought and speech, said to the scholastic professors of his day:

"Inasmuch as the very pinnacle of ignorance is taking doubtful things for certain, I beseech you, let us for one moment think, suppose, pretend that we are thorough ignoramuses. Perhaps we shall gain in wisdom and insight, if we find that hitherto we have been taking darkness—or at any rate faint twilight glimmerings—for noonday. Then we shall either go back to our first opinion, and hold it much more firmly than before; or else we shall recognise that we were blind, and exchange it for a better." (In St. Cyres' *Pascal*, p. 39.)

We have no right to denounce the views of others until we have exposed ourselves to their attraction and understood why they have proved persuasive to their minds. The sharing of intellectual difficulties is an exhausting experience. One must make one's self start from other people's premises, however stupid and silly they may seem, and think along with them, if possible, into the marvellous light of the Gospel.

It is so in the sanctuary of sympathy—both with joy and with sorrow, and how rapid for ministers are the transitions from one to the other! A wedding may follow upon a funeral with only an hour's interval. If you can go to the house of mourning and come away undrained, it is fairly certain that no virtue of comfort went out of you. You did not feel what its inmates were feeling. There is a penetrating and scathing diagnosis of much that passes for sympathy in the comment of a young woman of an earlier generation:

"The sympathy of most people consists of a mixture of good humor, curiosity and self-importance."

That should get under the skin of those of us who have become professionalized. Nor should we forget that to be a companion of those in pain or grief is no light task. The nurse of the woesome Phaedra in Euripides' *Hippolytus* says:

"Oh, pain were better than tending pain!
For that were single, and this is twain,
With grief of heart and labor of limb."

Do you recall the moving scene in *A Tale of Two Cities* where in the French Revolution a man is giving up his life for a friend and finds himself riding in the death-cart to the guillotine beside a mere girl, who says to him:

"If I may ride with you, may I hold your hand?
I am not afraid, but I am little and weak, and it will give more courage."

They rode together. No fear was in her eyes. She looked at the composed face beside her, and said:

"I think you were sent to me by Heaven."

Such heavenly ministries of courage take a vast lot out of the God-sent minister.

And there is the sanctuary of shame for sin. In the congregation where I served for many years on the East Side of New York, a boy in the Sunday School, who had been taken into a gang of youths a bit older than himself, had been involved in a series of robberies and was in the Tombs prison. When I went to see him, he begged me not to let his Sunday School teacher know of his misdoing: "He will take it too hard." So must it always be with those who minister in the name of One who took our griefs, carried our sorrows, and bore our sins on His conscience and in His own body on the tree. When he was holding his meetings for medical students in Edinburgh, Henry Drummond was staying with friends of mine in Charlotte Square. One night he came back, and, when standing by the mantel looking very worn and white, the friend said to him:

"Are you sick?"
"Yes, sick of the sins of these men. How does God stand them?"

Oliver Goldsmith wrote of the village pastor:

"He watched and wept and prayed *and felt for all.*

This is the drain to which sons of Kohath must expect to be subjected to whom belongs the service of the sanctuary.

But they never minister alone. And He who shares it with them is a fountain of living water. In and from Him they are renewed and refreshed and restored in soul. It is fuller, not depleted, selves which they are enabled to present as living sacrifices unto God.

4

THE CRAFTSMANSHIP
OF THE MONSTRANCE

WE HAVE used as the sub-title of these chapters
Dr. Carnegie Simpson's suggestive metaphor for
preaching—the monstrance of the Gospel. It serves
to keep in view the main point that a sermon exalts
God in Christ for worship that He may enter into
personal fellowship with listeners. A monstrance,
if Protestants may venture into a realm alien to our
conceptions of the Gospel, is a creation on which
art and workmanship are naturally lavished that it
may worthily contain the Divine within. To our
minds it may seem that what is usually an ornate
implement ill comports with the ordinariness of the
symbols which our Lord employed in the acted
parable of His death and of His own meaning to
His disciples—the common loaf and the wine on
a Jewish family table. But when such a meal be-

comes the central event in a public ceremony and the focal point for the adoration of an assembly in solemn worship, it is not surprising that the monstrance containing the sacramental symbol and exhibiting it receives the adornment of aesthetic taste and skilled artisanship.

An evangelist shows us the pains which our Lord took in selecting a fitting metaphor in which to present His message of God's reign. We are taken into His careful preparation, and permitted to overhear Him thinking with Himself:

"Whereunto shall we liken the kingdom of God or with what comparison shall we compare it?"

The evangelist catches Him, so to speak, in the act of composition. The Gospel is truth not to be defined in a proposition but to be set forth to capture imagination and feeling as well as mind. Jesus must put it into a picture which shall charm and reveal. He is facing the task of providing a monstrance for His Gospel.

All art (and the art of sermon construction is no exception) is a struggle with formlessness—that original chaos into which our earth and all things in it, human thought and speech included—seem always eager to slip back. There is a widespread notion that divine truth is of itself so vitalizing and the Scriptures from which we derive it so charged with the inspiring Spirit that any sincere thought, however conventional, and any language, however dull, will serve for a sermon. To be sure the last thing wanted is self-conscious artistry. It was said of a brilliant Frenchwoman: "Elle s'écoute quand elle parle." There are preachers of whom one has that impression. They appear to listen to themselves and to derive considerable satisfaction from their performance. One almost hears an inward "Ah" at a clever epigram or a striking metaphor. It is well that a sermon should be interesting to someone, even if it be only its preacher. Its thought can rarely astonish by its singularity. The Gospel is no novelty to a congregation of reasonably regular church-goers. But there are preachers who take the old, old story and, by their luminous thinking and the color and savor of their words, compass the miracle of creating a work of art through which the living God clutches at our hearts and stabs our consciences.

As the artificer of a monstrance must be a con-noiseur in silver or gold, in patterns and tracery, in the precious stones with which he studs the vessel to reflect from their surfaces the glint and lustre which intimate the glory of the Divine enshrined within, so must a preacher fashion a sermon whose structure suggests Most High God in Christ, and whose words by their gleam and glow amaze and fascinate, arousing reverence and affection. In his form and language he is seeking to add loveliness to

clearness, to communicate the unfathomable greatness of God evoking wonder and wooing to passionate loyalty. He must have a sensitive feeling
for words. In World War II a host of public
speakers on the allied side said pretty much the
same things; but it was given to Winston Churchill
a master of language, as with a trumpet to rouse
millions to a pitch of courage and resolve. A member of the House of Commons, who was a loyal
follower of both Neville Chamberlain and Winston
Churchill, has this to say of their speaking during
the war:

"When Mr. Chamberlain said the fine true
thing, it was like a faint air played on a pipe and
lost on the wind at once. When Mr. Churchill said
it, it was like an organ filling the church, and we all
went out refreshed and resolute to do or die."
(*The Independent Member*, by A. P. Herbert,
1951, p. 120.)

If the traditions and liberties of a nation require
such apt and deft utterance to quicken and enlist
a people's might, and if God's gift to the free world
was the imagination and literary skill of a Churchill,
surely the Gospel of the glorious God in Christ demands like spokesmen, to assert its sway over our
generation and to marshal the Church to a victorious
advance on the part of threatened and despairing
men to secure for themselves and mankind the in-

domitable liberty with which Christ enfranchises.
Our monstrance is composed of a few sentences and
paragraphs strung together, but how resolutely
must preachers give themselves to acquire the taste
for the lovely and the command of thought and
speech to supply the means for embodying God's
Self-manifestation.

Our chief quarry is the Bible. Here in various
literary forms are books which generations have
found enabling God to meet them. They have all
proved themselves monstrances disclosing His presence or they would not have been included in the
Church's canon. It is no pulpit convention which
requires a text from Scripture. It is the effort to recapture for our messages today the supreme quality of revealing God. A preacher who does not
zealously collect texts from the Scriptures in order
to achieve in his time what the Biblical authors have
so conspicuously achieved does not belong in the
apostolic succession.

A monstrance must catch and hold the attention
of a congregation. No doubt the manner and bear-
ing of him who upraises it enhance or lessen its
arresting quality; but in addition it must inherently
possess this gripping property. Hence the danger
of employing texts which have become pulpit-worn.
Take a few curiosity-awakening Bible expressions—
"This is that," the three words in Peter's sermon at
Pentecost. The gift of the Spirit has been our antici-

23492

pation: here it is! "Me ye have not always," Jesus' defence of a woman's extravagant affection; "Have ye experienced so many things in vain?" Paul's question to the Galatians; "in his own person my very heart," the apostle's characterization of Onesimus as the American Revised Version translates it—an excellent Christmas text—these short phrases grip alert minds and open up at once the train of thought the sermon will pursue. One is spared introductory sentences and can leap at once into the message.

Kipling assured us that "there are nine and sixty ways of constructing tribal lays," and there are no fewer methods of making a sermon, as the history of Christian preaching renders clear. Getting started is always most important. If the attention of a congregation is securely captured and held down in the first few sentences, the preacher is well on his way to a message. A text and introduction which stick in my memory were used by the late Dr. George A. Gordon of the Old South Church, Boston. His text was "The devils also believe and tremble" and Gordon began:

"This fact I have always regarded as highly creditable to the devils. They had sense enough to believe, and they had conscience enough to fear. Our devils are in a worse plight. They neither believe nor tremble. That is vastly to their intellectual and moral discredit. It shows them to be much lower down in the scale of existence than the beings to whom reference is made in the text; it shows them to be nearly without sense and almost without conscience.

"My purpose is to read a lesson from the demons of St. James. Ministers are sometimes accused of preaching over the heads of their congregations, of selecting ideal persons and deducing the laws of life for ordinary mortals from the veritable saints and heroes of mankind. There can be no such complaint against the subject for today. The beings about whom I am to reason are, to put it mildly, hardly up to our level."

(In *Through Men to God*.)

With just a subtle touch of humor, and with an intriguing approach, he takes hold of the congregation and draws them to go with him.

Sometimes an illustration makes a catching opening. Do you recall Job's justification for keeping on praying when he feels that God has become his relentless enemy? "Howbeit doth not one stretch out the hand in his fall?" (Job 30:24 in a correct translation.) This is the compelling instinct of self-preservation, as true in the spiritual as in the physical life. Suppose one begins with the passage in Stevenson's *Ebb-Tide*, where Herrick, the derelict, trying to drown himself, finds that he cannot do it:

"The shock of the immersion brightened his mind immediately; the events of the ignoble day passed before him in a frieze of pictures; and he thanked 'whatever gods may be' for that open door of suicide. . . . Here, let him drop the curtain, let him seek the ineffable refuge, let him lie down with all races and generations of men in the house of sleep. It was easy to say, easy to do. To stop swimming—there was no mystery in that, if he could do it. Could he? And he could not. He knew it instantly. He was aware instantly of an opposition in his members, unanimous and invincible, clinging to life with a single and fixed resolve, finger by finger, sinew by sinew; something that was at once he, and not he; at once within and without him. . . . To any man there may come at times a consciousness that there blows through all the articulations of his body the wind of a spirit not wholly his; that his mind rebels; that another girds him and carries him whither he would not. It came now to Herrick. The open door was closed in his recreant face."

Spiritual self-destruction is equally difficult. There is something in the structure of man's soul which clings to God. After the death of his wife, Sir Leslie Stephen, answering Mr. Lowell's letter of condolence, began a sentence, "I thank" and suddenly recalled that as an agnostic he must not write the word "God"; so the letter stands "I thank —something—that I loved her as heartily as I know how to love." (*Life & Letters*, p. 256.)

Analogies from the physical to the spiritual make excellent beginnings, for, as our Lord knew, we men are immersed in the material world and the spiritual gives an impression of apparent unreality. Suppose one is preaching on faith, and using for a text the two words so frequent in Hebrews 11, "by faith," one may begin with the remark that connectives discharge an essential function in our universe. Then instance chlorophyll which links the vegetable world to the source of life and energy in the sun. "By chlorophyll grass, shrubs, trees are clad in green and furnished power to grow." Then instance hemoglobin in our blood, which links bodies with oxygen, "the breath of life" in the atmosphere, aerates the system, and supplies energy by which we think, move, and act. "By hemoglobin our bodies possess vigor for life's work." Similarly faith links men with the Fountain of Life in God. Then go on to show what it enabled those listed in that chapter to achieve and endure. Beginning with the obviously actual, that sense of actuality carries over into a realm which to many seems vague and nebulous.

There is always a peril that when we start off with a Biblical text we seem to be dealing with ancient history and not with that which is urgently contemporary. We may well begin with a few sentences which portray our present plight, and then bring in a Biblical situation where identical or similar circumstances dominate the scene. The text is lifted at once out of the remote past and made relevant to today. Many preachers feel the Biblical material hampering, so they dispense with it almost entirely at the outset and only introduce it incidentally later on. Hence the popularity of topical as opposed to textual sermons. The peril in this method is that we cut off our message from the historic Self-revelation of God which the Church of the centuries has garnered in the Scriptures, and that (without being aware of it) we are preaching what is questionably Christian.

A congregation assembled for worship comes together on certain assumptions, and he who leads them should respect the mutual basis on which he and they meet. They are not there to listen to the ideas of a speaker, however interesting, but to share the heritage of the Church of all the Christian centuries. The preacher is an authorized and commissioned representative of the Church as well as a personal ambassador of God in Christ. Through all the acts of public worship—hymns, prayers, Scripture lessons, the architecture and atmosphere of the edifice—the congregation enters on the inheritance and the present fellowship of the Church visible and invisible. The sermon must possess this quality which renders it God's venerable and ageless Gospel. Scripture pre-eminently conveys this quality and communicates it to the minister's timely message rendering it the eternal truth of Him who is from everlasting to everlasting.

Some ministers scoff at the habit of taking a Bible "tag" as a necessary basis for a sermon. Let me counter by urging that we employ much longer passages of Scripture and thus make it plain that we are attempting to give the message of the historic Self-disclosure of God as the foundation for our message today. Take the Revelation of St. John, admittedly an obscure book and surrendered by too many ministers to the "fringe sects" who fairly camp in it for their often fantastic versions of the Gospel. It is the first full-length Christian interpretation of history, and most relevant to our age. Suppose one starts with the vision in the fifth chapter of a book written on both sides of its pages and close sealed—the book of destiny. Then undertake in twenty-five minutes to summarize the entire *Revelation* so that its conviction of God's reign in history holds men in the present. It can be done under four points:

1. The certain downfall of the dominant secular culture. Rome, then all-powerful, is viewed by this prisoner in one of her concentration camps as doomed. "She glorified herself"—the fatal self-sufficiency of all secularism. "Strong is the Lord God which judged her."

2. The continuing instability to be expected when a great culture breaks up. There is a middle stretch in this book—chapters six through sixteen—

which usually bores any reader who goes through
the book at a sitting with its monotonously recurring
disasters. First the seven seals, each (as it is broken)
unloosing a catastrophe. Then when one thinks
every woe imaginable has been undergone, seven
angels step forward with their trumpets, and at the
blast of each angel new calamities occur. With the
seventh trumpet one may fancy nothing more de-
structive remains in store; but seven bowls are
emptied on hapless humanity. Here is a profound
insight into history. When a civilization collapses—
like the Roman Empire or the industrial world of
nineteenth- and early twentieth-century Europe and
America—tranquillity is not soon regained. Earth
reels under blow on blow. This is not good news
to our generation, but it is God's truth and must be
faced. Christians must prepare themselves to take
it and take it and take it again.

3. The Church, through which God carries out
His main purpose in history, is represented in
chapters two and three by seven flickering lamps
shining against the black darkness of a doomed
world. Its members are a very mixed body of
Christians, certainly not conspicuously better than
those of the weakest churches of our day. The two
qualities the seer demands of them are faith and
steadfastness. Faith sees, as in chapter four and
following, another and heavenly world open, where
God reigns and ten thousand times ten thousand

share His triumph. This view must always be within the prospect of Christians, who, whatever the clangor of an earth in conflict, hear the confident chorus of the redeemed:

"Hallelujah: for the Lord our God the Almighty reigneth. Let us rejoice and be exceeding glad."

Such faith produces steadfastness—the endurance which is able to "take it" as a reeling earth brings us crisis upon crisis.

4. The climax of history is the arrival of the city of God. It does not emerge as the development of the trends and happenings in history. The evolutionary theory is not the Biblical interpretation of the course of events. It holds an adventist theory: this world is God's; He made it and is always acting in it. But it becomes recalcitrant and thwarts His purpose. He then arrives in judgment and in redemption. Christians think of His coming in Jesus. History will conclude in another such Coming. That is our hope—not of a commonwealth marred by human ignorances and sin, but of a society whose architect and builder is God. This does not imply that all men's strivings are to be scrapped as of no lasting worth: into the city from heaven are brought the glory and honor of the nations, but the social fabric is God's and descends from Him out of heaven. And if one asks what is this heavenly

society like, the answer is subsumed briefly: "The throne of God and of the Lamb shall be in it." Life is completely harmonious with the will of God manifest in Jesus of Calvary. And what of its citizens? Three things are plainly said: They are useful—"His servants shall serve Him"; they are companionable, companionable with God and therefore with one another—"they shall see His face"; their characters reflect clearly the Divine—"His name shall be in their foreheads." This society is the end product of human history, the fulfilment of the purpose of the incoming and always active God.

A single sermon may make these points and apply them to fill the current horizon. The Book of Revelation is no blueprint of events in today or tomorrow; it is an interpretation of the course of history under the reign of God in every epoch. It stands at the conclusion of the Christian Bible as a glorious monstrance of the Gospel of His redeeming sovereignty through His Church in the affairs of mankind. Its sublime assurance stems from that opening vision of the Son of man, the First and the Last, in the secrets of the Eternal and with the final word on human events, who was dead, and is alive forevermore, and holds the keys to the overwhelming mysteries. He has overcome the world, and calls on us to be fellow-conquerors through Him and share His victorious life.

One may similarly take an entire Gospel and set forth its distinctive contribution to our portrait of Jesus; or one may take an epistle and bring out its interpretation of the Christian life. Who is the Christ of St. Paul, and what manner of men are His servants? Who is the Christ of the Johannine Epistles and with what faith and love do Christians appear in this world? This is not to take Biblical "tags"; but to open up New Testament vistas. And the same can be done for Old Testament prophets, psalmists and wise men. A preacher may use the books of Nahum and of Jonah as contrasting sermons on the same event—the fall of Nineveh—the one a cry of vengeance and the other an insistence on the forgiveness of the righteous and sovereign God. Each Old Testament book has its particular religious message. It is a shame that so few among even our most faithful church-goers know what these messages are. The blame lies with us preachers who so rarely are, like Apollos, "mighty in the Scriptures." We complain that our people do not read their Bibles. Do we open up for them the riches of the books and whet their curiosity to explore them and become possessors of their treasures of wisdom and knowledge?

If the foundation of a man's preaching is the Bible, that foundation usually suggests the outline of his sermon. It is possible, of course, to impose an outline on a text or on a longer passage. This is likely to be artificial and mechanical. As a rule the Biblical material seems to throw out salient points, and around and under them the contents of a sermon take their place. Once get well started under the lead of a Bible verse or a Bible book and the sermon seems to move of its own accord. To be sure, one has to learn the art of omission. One's aim is not to do justice to all that is in a text, but to use its main message for the inspiration of the men and women to whom one is speaking. They can take so much and no more at a sitting, and one does well to recall that Sundays recur once a week and many of us have midweek meetings besides. Not everything must be crammed into one half-hour period, but enough to let the God and Father of Jesus Christ appear in His august graciousness.

A preacher must collect illustrations as systematically as he collects texts, and must employ them with a skill that makes them illustrate his message, and not become either so absorbing or so opaque that listeners recall them rather than the Gospel. A monstrance has a glass window through which the emblem of deity within looks forth. That is the sole function of an illustration. Whatever it may be—an incident, a remark, a current happening, some lines of verse, a character in a book, a principle derived from the world of nature—its only role in a sermon is to supply an opening through which men look in on God and He can look forth on them. The glass in a monstrance is transparent and is instantly forgotten. What is within claims and holds worshippers' undivided attention. Test any illustration by that small pane of glass. While of itself the glass makes no claim on interest, still it must be there or the monstrance is not properly a monstrance showing forth the sacramental symbol. An unillustrated sermon is equally no monstrance. It does not stimulate the imagination by which alone the unseen becomes actual to us. Remember again our Lord in His preparation to preach:

"Whereunto shall we liken the kingdom of God? or with what comparison shall we compare it?"

It is written of our Lord that "the common people heard Him gladly." That is not true of many in the pulpit today. Our churches are rarely filled with men from carpenter's shops and factory benches, with miners and taxi drivers. One wonders how much the average man or woman with no more than grammar school education gets out of most sermons. A minister has to expurgate his vocabulary of technical words, of words of more than two syllables such as "expurgate," "vocabulary," "technical" which have just been employed, of words which for lack of gripping power do not lay hold of the minds of plain folk. But important as this is, it is the picturesqueness of a minister's thought and speech which counts supremely. Preaching to boys and girls is the best kind of training for preaching to adults. Few adults are more than adolescent in mind, and in current appeals to them everything is scaled down to early adolescence. Listen to any radio program. One is aware that for children the Christian message must turn their ears into eyes if they are to see it. In sermons to boys and girls, supposedly of riper years but rarely of maturer intelligence, sentences must be of imagination all compact. Nothing would be more educational for most ministers than to be asked to address chance audiences on street corners or in public parks and interest them in spiritual truth. It was with such audiences that Christian preaching began in the early Church, and with such audiences that the Church gets its start again on mission fields. It is invaluable to acquire the power of mastering attention, of developing thought from point to point and ramming home the main lessons, and above all of leading up to a decisive conclusion and stopping instantly. A decorous congregation will let a minister continue when he has said all he has to say; a chance group on the street corner will turn and go their several ways.

These chapters are not the occasion to go into the details of building up a sermon and arriving at a cogent conclusion. Let me take time to pass on one counsel given recently to speakers in the House of Commons by A. P. Herbert, an editor of *Punch* as well as a statesman. Although a master of speech he found addressing the House so difficult that he calls it "the torture chamber."

"For one thing the unprepared one has not thought how he is going to end, and tends to wander about in search of the exit. If you prepare nothing else, my boy, be sure that you know how you are going to end."

(*The Independent Member*, by A. P. Herbert, 1951, p. 52.)

The art of effective sermon-writing is toilsome, and each man has to learn for himself with painstaking effort how to communicate truth persuasively and convincingly. For every hearer, learned and less learned, simplicity and plainness of thought and language are essential. University congregations, faculty and students alike, as well as street corner audiences, appreciate the picturesque. To Nicodemus no less than to the crowds by the lake or on the hillside, Jesus put his thought into metaphors. "Without a parable spake He not unto them."

But today in this country we speak to congregations who possess more formal education than any preceding generation. The chief difficulty with most sermons is that they lack sufficient content and do not convey what they have with sufficient precision to hold the thinking of their listeners. Given a minister possessed by the Gospel in its breadth and depth, and men recognize that he has enough to say, and usually they listen to him. Suffer me to refer to one who laid his mind on me in student days and on many more students and ministers in subsequent years.

In the 1890's, in my second year at New College, Edinburgh, W. M. Macgregor began his ministry at Free St. Andrews, a very sparsely attended church in the heart of the city's West End. He had a striking appearance in the pulpit, with a profile which suggested the bust of Dante. From voice and speech and style, it was clear that he was an intellectual aristocrat, with broad culture, a multifarious reading from which he drew apt quotations to drive home his points. He seemed austere, scrupulously exact in thought and language, and he spoke with an unforgettable voice, measured, unhurried, and with a plaintive note in it, wistful and haunting as the cry of a curlew from his native highlands. His prayers were profoundly moving with depth and insight and with understanding both of man in his frailty and of the heights of God towards which he aspires. When he preached, his language was so painstakingly chosen that listeners were on the alert for every word, and every word counted in the accurate expression of his thought. He seemed to have put his sentences through a wringer before he set them down, or perhaps after he had written them, to squeeze out every otiose word. His was a lean style, and it made exciting listening. He was a profound Biblical scholar, using his Hebrew and Greek and giving often his own translations of passages, and he led us into the full reaches of the Scriptures with which he dealt. Everything seemed to be fresh and real. There were no threadbare ideas, no hackneyed similes, no conventional piety. His words had cutting edges. It was not popular preaching, drawing throngs, for it made too exacting a demand upon intelligence. But there was nothing like it at the time, and probably since, in that city of notable preachers. One watched the congregation grow slowly; but what it lacked in numbers was compensated for in weight. Seldom could one see so many professional men—barristers, writers to the signet, university professors, and especially ministers who had run up for a week-end in Edinburgh. Invariably the congregation was led to face God in His sovereign holiness and in His loving kindness. It was a vision which awed and attracted. Macgregor presented us with the *Mysterium tremendum et fascinosum,* of which Rudolf Otto was later to write. My fellow student, Arthur Gossip, applies to Macgregor, Faber's lines:

"For his one thought was God,
  In that one thought he abode,
  Forever in that thought more deeply sinking."

In the early years of our century the publishing firm of T. & T. Clark projected a series of volumes of sermons under the caption *The Scholar As Preacher*, and persuaded Macgregor to let them have material for one in their first series. At once he leapt to fame in the British Islands. Journeymen ministers, hard put to it to produce two discourses a Sunday, found enough in one of his to set their minds off on profitable paths. Like Robertson of Brighton, he became a preachers' preacher. For a whole generation he made an enriching impression upon the pulpit of his native land and a wider public. Small wonder that the General Assembly took him to its Glasgow college to fill the New Testament chair, and later elected him its principal.

Let me quote a few sentences from a sermon on the text:

"All we like sheep have gone astray, we have turned everyone to his own way; and the Lord hath laid on him the iniquity of us all."

(In *Jesus Christ, The Son of God*, Edinburgh.)

Macgregor says:

"Many estimable people are travelling on through life without a suspicion of offense, doing what others do and judging as others judge—like sheep; and it never occurs to them to ask if their world has room in it for the Cross, in which they profess to believe. Actually they do not need it, and they do not understand it. Walter Bagehot, in one place, speaks of 'those gentlemen who revolt from what is coarse, are sickened by what is gross, hate what is ugly. The law in their members does not war against the law in their minds. They live within the hedgerows of polished society, and they do not wish to go beyond them into the great deep of human life,' and then abruptly he adds 'These are the men whom it is hardest to make Christians.'"

Macgregor goes on to speak of the woes and sins of men flocking to Christ:

"He treated them as no intrusion. His chosen business was to bear the inflictions which have come upon the world of men, acknowledging them as righteous, and thus to bring hope and pardon to the hopeless. . . . Some writers have magnified the pathos of the Cross, a beautiful soul broken by the bigotry and selfishness of men; and some have extolled the heroism of it, a creature greatly daring who would not, by any threat be turned aside from delivering his message, who, in the agony of death, thinking only of that, shouts, like a conqueror, 'It is finished.' These give occasions for spirited writing, but they only bring us to the beginning. To see the inner necessity of the Cross, how He laid it on Himself, and made offering of Himself through an Eternal Spirit—that is the real interpretation; and the power that changes lives is there. 'He loved me, and gave Himself for me.'"

The lucidity of both thought and language, the utter fitness of the quotation, the packed content of every sentence holding one's thoughtful attention, make a monstrance which rivets worshipful minds and focusses them upon Christ in His constraining and astonishing love—the everlasting Gospel.

One may criticise preaching patently over the heads of the multitude; but there ought surely to be some pulpits which satisfy educated and mature listeners. We cannot forget that every year many more young people go through college. This by no means guarantees that they become intelligent and thoughtful. But many of them are, and many more without college training are so also, and it is heartbreaking that there are so few preachers who feed both minds and hearts and gratify the love of beauty. Where, even in a great city, have you a preacher to whom you may confidently send an intellectually and spiritually mature person, assuring him that he will be abundantly fed? A few such pulpits raise the general level, keep the Church of God in a commanding position with men who think, and provide the enlightening leadership requisite if the Church is to guide a generation into the fullness of the mind of Christ. Protestantism has sought to offer its people a reasonable worship. It has set out to produce Christians who use their minds in their intercourse with the Most High. God is light as well as love, and our bewildered day desperately needs sons of light, patently children of God's day. The pulpit as well as her system of Christian education has been the Church's chief means of bringing such followers of Christ into being. Its occupants must study to be shining, as well as burning, lights. Her ministers must be passionate devotees of truth, and so dedicated to it that they insist upon its precise and persuasive utterance—a monstrance congruous with the Gospel in which they believe and setting it forth convincingly.

The design of monstrances is usually cruciform. The essence of the Gospel is Christ crucified. "He bare our sins," says a humbly grateful Church. But that verb puzzles many present-day Christians. What did Christ bear at Calvary?

He bore the malignant *force* of the evils of society in His anguished body. The traditionalism of churchmen, the greed of the possessors of economic privilege, the opportunism of a politician in authority, the frivolity of a playboy, Herod, who decked Him in mock royalty and made game of Him, the emotional hysteria of a mob, the bitterness of a disillusioned idealist, the unquestioning obedience of regimented soldiers, the apathy of the public, the racial and nationalistic snobbery which chose a degrading and brutal form of execution for one who belonged to an inferior people—these forces are all present and active in His death. This is our world.

These sinister factors are all alive and dominant in our society. This is *ourselves*—for they all live in and move us.

Again he bore the burdening *pressure* of sin on His conscience. Why is He there in that religious capital exposed to murderous enemies? The sense of social obligation which at the Jordan insisted on receiving the symbol of repentance for a nation's sins sounds in the saying: "The Son of man must suffer and be killed." His conscience was "a nerve o'er which do creep the else unfelt oppressions of the earth."

In World War II, a brave company of anti-Hitler Germans conspired to overthrow Nazism and cleanse their nation of its soiling sway. They found out that the Gestapo knew their intentions, but they refused the chance to flee as treachery to duty; and all save one of them paid the penalty of death. So Jesus endured the Just for the unjust.

Again He bore the *confusion* of sin in His mind. How account for the bewilderment in Gethsemane: "If it be possible"; "now is the power of darkness," He said. One sees that baffling darkness in His words to the weeping women. His death will bring on the destruction of His and their loved city and the appalling slaughter of numbers of women and children. Life's decisions have in them this criss-cross of conflicting consequences. Should He persevere and be the cause of such stark woe? A sympathetic interpreter writes: "He suffered, being tempted." Try to enter that tortured mind: Was He making a mistake? He was laying down His life an emancipation for many, but were there many, indeed were there any, who would be affected by it? "If thou hadst *known*," He had said with tears to Jerusalem. Would she ever know? Was He jeopardizing Himself and His cause in vain? All His reliance was on God; but He questioned His faithfulness. If God abandoned Him, what prospect of an emancipation for many was there in His sacrifice? There are

> "Fallings from us, vanishings,
>   Blank misgivings of the creature."

"He suffered, being tempted."

Again He bore on His heart the *shame* of those who slew Him. Who were they? His kinsmen in the family of God, and they were reddening their hands with the blood of their Father's representative. The vitality of the characters in His parables comes from His having *been* all these people—the hungry and self-loathing son in the far country, the waiting father, the sheep "harassed and helpless," who evoked His compassion. "He who lives more lives than one, more deaths than one must die." He was torn between recoil and revulsion from the men who compassed His death—Caiaphas, Pilate, Judas, the staring and mocking crowd—and a feeling of oneness with them, His brethren. "For them that were sick, I was sick"; for them who by their obtuseness derided God, I was ashamed.

Again He bore sins *away*. What a contrast between the page where heart-broken followers watch Him die, and say to one another: "We trusted that it had been He which should have redeemed," and the page where an innumerable company praise Him "who loved us and loosed us from our sins in His own blood." A newspaper editor went to see the Passion Play at Oberammergau, and came away saying to himself: "This is the story which has transformed the world"; and he seemed to hear an echo from the Bavarian mountains: "Yes, and will transform it." "Behold the Lamb of God, which taketh away the sin of the world."

This is the Gospel which the monstrance of our preaching must hold up plainly before congregations. It will tax our brains to put it enlighteningly. It will drain our lives to set it forth movingly.

One may object that in this chapter too much emphasis is being placed on the artistry of preaching. You recall Carlyle's biting comment on a notable London preacher: "If he had anything to say, he would know how to say it." The technique was there, but no imperative tidings. And yet the message without corresponding technique becomes obscure and impotent. An artist of the last century, Sir Edward Burne-Jones, exalting his calling, wrote:

"That was an awful word of Ruskin's that artists paint God for the world. There's a lump of greasy pigment at the end of Michelangelo's hog-bristle brush, and by the time it has been laid on the stucco, there is something that all men with eyes recognize as Divine. Think what it means: it is the power of bringing God into the world—making God manifest."

That is the miracle of our calling. A few skillfully chosen words—thoughts clearly in line with the mind of Christ—a man speaking earnestly of that which has mastered him, and there is something heard that all men with ears recognize as Divine. Think what it means: it is the power of letting God become manifest.